Copyright©Chris Reid *Heirlooms and Hand-me-downs*

First published 2011
By Dublin City Council

Chris Reid has asserted his moral rights
chrisreidartist.com

ISBN: 978-0-9554281-4-2

All rights reserved: The material in this publication is protected by copyright law. Except as may be permitted by law, no part of the material may be reproduced (including by storage in a retrieval system) or transmitted in any form or by any means: adapted, rented or lent without the written permission of the copyright owner and individual participants. Permission will normally be given to voluntary and community sector organisations except for commercial purposes.

Opinions expressed in *Heirlooms and Hand-me-downs* are the contributors' own and not necessarily shared by Dublin City Council and Create.

Cover: Five children who lived in Bride Street in the 1940s. Back (left to right): David McFadden, Fergus Redmond, Seán Redmond. Front (left to right): Marie Redmond, Irene Redmond. Photo courtesy of Fergus Redmond.

Design by Zinc
Printed in Ireland by DCK Ebrook

Stories from Nicholas Street, Bride Street, Bride Road and the Rosser, Dublin

By Chris Reid

Contents

Introduction	6
Location	8
A Public History of Community and Place Inspired by Private Voices	10

1900-1930 — 16
Father	18
Letters From France	22
Union	24
Rebels	25
Grandmother	26
Mark of a Bullet	29
The Suitcase	29
Civil War	30
Holes in His Legs	33
Moving House	36

1930s — 38
Eucharistic Congress	40
Processions	41
First Communion	43
Play	43
What Your Mother Said Was Law	45
We Didn't Have Locks	46
Childhood Illness	47
Getting a Job	49
They Passed Remarks	49

1940s — 52
Faith of Our Fathers, and Mothers	54
Sunshine House	56
My Father's Voice	57
Work Inside and Outside The Home	57
Quaker Style Care For Workers	59
Net Curtains and White Sheets	60
Tenement House Collapses	63
Moving From The Tenements	63
War Stories-Sent Out	64
Table Manners	66
Rations	67
The Telegram Boy	68
Censored Letters	68
Another Letter	69
He Had Enough Memories	69
He Wouldn't Talk About it	70
Demobbed	70
Home Front	70
Minding Big Houses	72

Uncle	73
A Good Social Life	74
Family Planning	77
I Was Very Innocent...	77
Irish in England	78
The Bayno-England in Ireland	80

1950s — 82
One of Thirteen	84
Games and Schools	84
Names and Unlocked Doors	85
I Grew Up on The Ross Road	85
Games	87
Two Pools	88
Rambling	89
The Sanatorium	89
The Tenements on High Street	90
Christmas Dinner	93
Flower	93
In His Latter Years	94
Girls' School	95
Saturday at the Iveagh Market	96
The Area-An Adventure Playground	98
The Bayno	98
Wild Children	100
Everybody Just Mingled	100
Snobbery and Poverty	102
Buckets of Slop and The Cinema	102
Gas Man	103
The Rag Man & Rag Woman	103
Running Battle on Francis Street	104
Boys School	106
Miraculous Medal and Sodalities	106
Inhibition	108
Hoolie	108
The Emigrant	110

1960s — 112
Horses and Henshaw's	114
Nancy on The Ross Road	114
Names and Premises Remembered	115
Babies and Prams	116
Hercules and The Invalidity Milk	117
I'd Get The Turf . . .	118
Chopping and Selling Sticks	118
Ma's Teeth	120
Wake	120
Climbing the Pipes	123

A Sad End To a Dance	123	Gas Explosion	173
We Shouldn't Have Jeered Her	124	Petty Crime	175
School Days	124	Iveagh Baths	177
Study	125	New Parking Meters	178
Me Father's Footsteps	126	New Resident	178
Saved From the Industrial Schools	126	The Store Detective	180
Daingean	128	Mother and Daughter	182
Altar Boys	129	Family Dispute	183
The Rat and The Nun	130	Leaving Home	184
Hoppers	131		
The Wringer	131	**1990s**	**186**
The Rag Man	132	Hand-me-downs	189
Heirlooms	134	The Swimmer	189
Work, Song - Opportunities	135	Thirty Years After	190
Joining The FCA, Earning Money	136	Regret	191
		New Flat	191
1970s	**138**		
Moggy	141	**2000s**	**196**
1 Ross Road - The Hall	141	Refurbishment	198
A Babysitting Barman	142	I Don't Know Anyone Now	198
Discos and Showbands	143	I Like It	199
Looking For a Job	143	New Yards, New Flats	201
Woolfson's Rag Stores	144	Local Pubs, Places, People	201
Washing Lines	145	Home	204
Loitering Cards, a Toss School	145	Familiar Foot, Strange Foot	204
Orphans	146	After The Renovation	204
Washing The Stairs	146	Refuge	206
Local Choir	148	Misunderstanding	206
Toss School in The Yard	148	Relationship	211
Letters From America	151	Dublin 2 or Dublin 8?	212
Relationships And The Flats	151	Living History	213
Fuel Donors	152	Grateful	213
Pubs-Places to Meet	153	Looking Back, Looking Forward	215
Paying Respects to Dev	155	I'm Fairly Happy But...	216
Lost Brother	157	Archaeology	217
Hard	157	The Balconies	217
The Lounge Boy	158		
Showbusiness Dreams	160	**Some Past Residents**	**218**
Joining The British Army	160	**Figure and Ground:**	
Marriage-An Escape	161	**Reflections on the Practice**	
My Grandmother	161	**of Chris Reid**	**220**
Boys' School	164	The Plaques	228
Mrs. Slyman	164	The Final 21 Plaques	232
		Credits	234
1980s	**166**	**Acknowledgements**	**235**
The Visit	168		
On Both Sides	171		
Dabbling	173		

Introduction

Heirlooms & Hand-me-downs is the final part of a Public Art Commission undertaken by artist Chris Reid in the Bride Street and Nicholas Street area of Dublin 8. The commission was funded through the *Per Cent for Art Scheme* by the Department of the Environment, Heritage and Local Government and related to the refurbishment of flat complexes in the area.

Chris Reid has engaged with the community of residents in the flats complex and collected stories, memories and photographs which have been fundamental to the commission. These stories which span almost a century have resulted in bronze texts with quotes from residents which are affixed to external walls of the flat complexes and in this publication *Heirlooms & Hand-me-downs*. The work has culminated in a deep insight into an inner city area of Dublin and the generosity of the residents in their participation is particularly appreciated.

Dublin City Council is delighted to have worked in partnership with Create, the national development agency for collaborative arts in bringing this publication to fruition.

Sinéad Connolly – Acting City Arts Officer, Dublin City Council

Chris Reid talks to John Slyman on Bride Street. Photo by Anthony Cassidy.

Heirlooms & Hand-me-downs

Location

Aerial photograph showing Nicholas Street, Ross Road, Bride Street, Bride Road and other connecting streets. This photo was taken in 1982.

1 Story No. 41 (Page 76)

8 Story No. 140 (Page 193)

15 Story No. 150 (Page 207)

2 (Page 202)

9 Story No. 129 (Page 176)

16 Story No. 116 (Page 156)

3 Stories 9/28/34/35 (Page 71)

10 (Page 58)

17 (Page 210)

4 Story No. 154 (Page 214)

11 Story No. 146 (Page 203)

18 Story No. 98 (Page 140)

5 (Page 233)

12 Story No. 94 (Page 133)

19 Story No. 144 (Page 200)

6 Story No. 40 (Page 75)

13 Stories 105/109 (Page 149)

20 Story No. 17 (Page 48)

7 (Page 91)

14 Story No. 107 (Page 147)

21 Stories 113/145 (Page 154)

8 ▬ The Poddle river runs underground through the area.

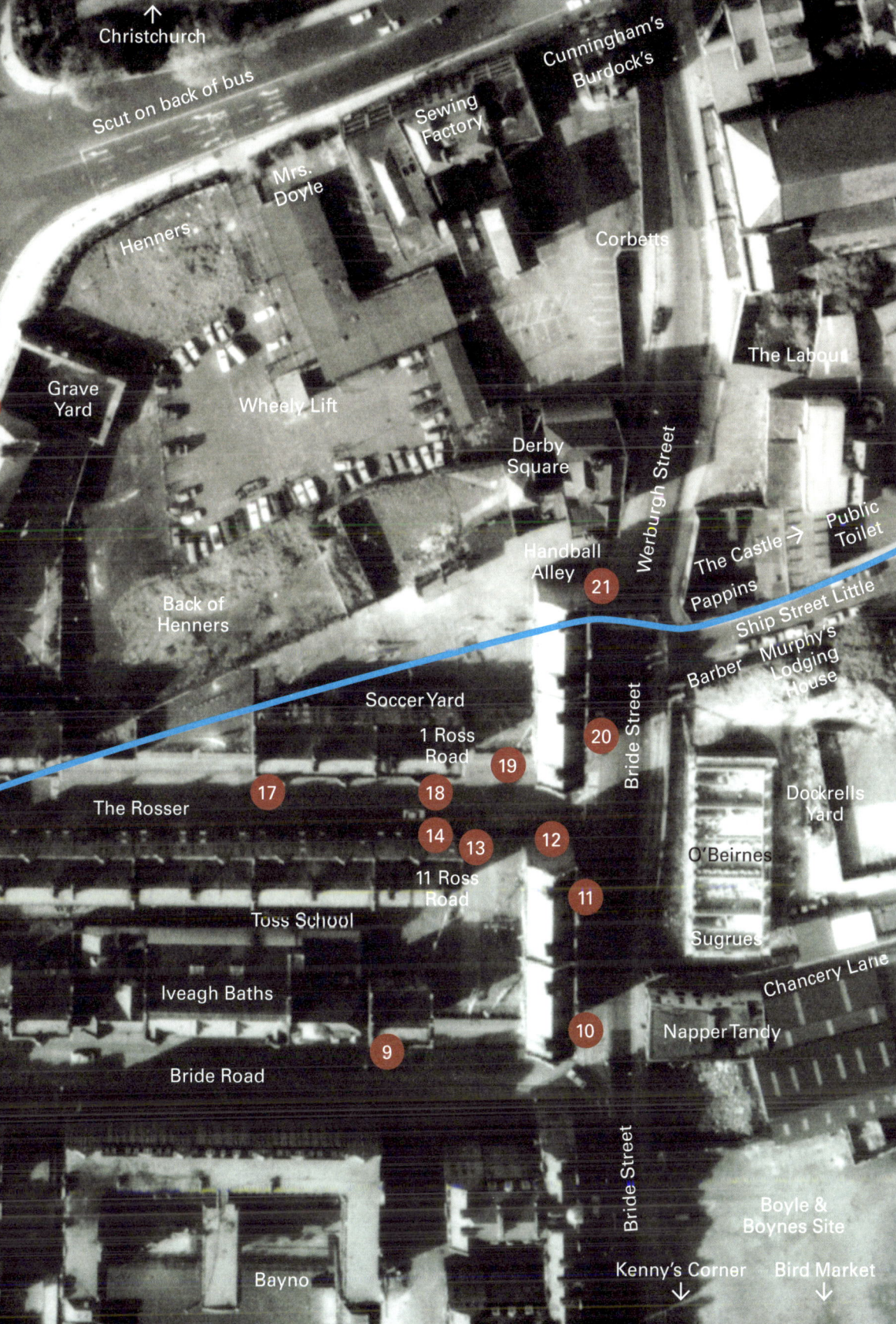

Heirlooms & Hand-me-downs

A Public History of Community and Place Inspired by Private Voices

The Liberties area in Dublin 8 is rich in history and heritage. Situated between Christchurch Cathedral and Saint Patrick's Cathedral, the Victorian three and four storey red brick flats on Nicholas Street, Ross Road, Bride Street and Bride Road are located along the tourist trail. Once slated for demolition, the flats have now been preserved on the grounds that they are a key part of Dublin's architectural heritage.

The flats were originally built as social housing in 1905 and though many residents have left over the years, after the refurbishment in the late 1990s, a number of residents still remain who are direct descendants of the original families.

Nicholas Street circa 1990s. Image courtesy of Kieran Kavanagh, Dublin City Architects Division.

Other residents have families living in the Liberties for many generations. It could be argued that through social and familial continuity, lived history can be transmitted from generation to generation through stories that trace experience of events and their consequences. However the voices of these local people are generally not heard or included in the heritage of the area.

With this reality in mind I set out to create a micro 'history' about Nicholas Street, Ross Road, Bride Street and Bride Road. This 'history' is based on audio recordings of conversations I had with residents and people associated with the area. These oral narratives formed the basis of a subjective local history and heritage that would be placed back into the area. This history would privilege the human reality of a given situation rather than any factual account. In effect *I wanted to create a public history of place through the private memories of its members.*

Gathering the material was difficult. It took time and patience. I tried many methods to meet people from cold calling on flats, to leafleting, to posing the question 'Would you like to be involved in telling the story of your area?'

Some of my attempts failed. Some people were reluctant to engage, some were happy to engage and provided a wealth of stories. Others engaged but were more circumspect, some wished to be anonymous. A couple of participants helped me out by providing contacts and even setting up 'interviews'. I also found that taking it easy and meeting people over time built trust and a network of contributors. Each meeting was different. The individual circumstances of each meeting had a shaping influence on each recording which in turn influenced the diversity of stories written up. I decided to stop recording when I had forty potential contributors.

The transcripts of the recordings were turned into 220 short texts. The contributors participated in the selection of twenty short texts for use on plaques. These were typeset to mimic formal commemorative plaques, individually cast in bronze and installed on the walls of the streets between seven and eight foot from the ground.

Recent memories formed the basis of some of the plaques and in some cases address issues that are important for the local residents. Altogether these plaques attempt to give historical significance to these local voices by making monuments to the ordinary, the personal and the often ephemeral experiences they describe. The 'texts' also intersect with larger histories – municipal, national and global. In addition they relate working class histories, histories of childhood and stories of the individual. The twenty-one plaques provide a permanent sculptural artwork that over time will become another feature of the place and memory of the local area.

Chris Reid chats to John Slyman during the installation of plaques by staff from Bronze Art Ltd., 2008. Photos by Anthony Cassidy.

This book expands on the narratives alluded to in the plaques and includes other constructed narratives that originated in the audio recordings made over a six-year period with local people. Through collating and editing this material I considered it important that the book reflects local vernacular and the familiarity of popular anecdotes.

Through this process of editing and textual bricolage my attempt was to express place as an interweaving of story and storytelling. Through close reading of the narratives the gender identity or politics of individual participants can be glimpsed. These are stories that are embedded into the very fabric of place, and at the same time honour the complexity of the individual life. Place is personalised, but is also shaped by many voices. This is a history of place told through the living memories of the residents.

The contradictions of place are borne out by various narratives disclosed. A female narrator remembers her father who fought in the British Army. A male narrator remembers his aunt who fought in Cumann na mBan on the republican side during the Irish Civil War.

The narrative histories collated in this book include edited transcriptions of interviews with people who live in the flats and adjoining streets. The stories and anecdotes you read in this book embody lived memories and experiences of working class people from Dublin 8 as well as some people who moved away from the area or emigrated. They illustrate the extent to which a local area is intimately connected to national and global history. People living in this area fought in both world wars, in the War of Independence and the Irish Civil War. The cost of participation is evident in the stories, often narratives of physical injury, emotional trauma and silence rather than glory. These experiences filter down through generations, with consequences abruptly disrupting the flow of anecdote, and disclosing harsh and bewildering truths. Narratives from childhood experience appear throughout, everything from games, adventures and play to punishment and abuse.

This working class history is a municipal history, and it is also, like most subaltern histories, a history of discontinuities – changes in work practices and local industries are experienced here as redundancy, recession, unemployment and emigration. Demoralisation and addiction – the close companions to a declining local and national economy – this too is a part of our history.

Many of the stories are concerned with everyday life played out as epic – the co-operation between women to bring in the washing or to maintain the halls, how people socialised, how people did their shopping and above all the ways in which people survived with humour, resilience and resourcefulness.

Some anecdotes tell how both childhood and adult lives have been shaped by a triumphal Catholicism and the consequences of this in the everyday. The residents had no safety net from economic and social turbulence; many stories describe hard times and getting by despite the numerous challenges. Issues appear, recede and disappear only to appear again in the next generation – generations of men joined the British Army or Royal Air Force. Some stories could not be included for reasons of sensitivity and privacy.

My role in gathering the material was underpinned by an ethical consideration for the contributors. As a witness and chronicler I have as far as possible involved the participants and sought to safeguard both the community and individual contributors from any unnecessary exposure.

The book also includes photographic material from personal collections, the City Archives and National Archives. Once again the contributors have participated in the selection of the visual material included.

Two plaques installed on Nicholas Street and Ross Road respectively. Chris Reid puts the finishing touches to a plaque on Bride Road. Photos by Anthony Cassidy.

Though I thought I could include in this book most of the stories that could not be put on the plaques I have been proven wrong, as there are endless stories to draw upon. Decisions regarding which stories to include in this book were driven by my desire to create an artwork/heritage based on material that I was given on the site (in this case primarily audio recordings of conversations I had with contributors but also photos and other visual materials). My decisions and interpretation of place were based on my own understanding of history. As with any interpretation it is partial. Though it is partial, it is a narrative about place/community as it has changed through time as told through the personal memories of those living in this place and within this history.

This book is intended as a gift returned to the community from which it came. I would like to take this opportunity to thank each and every one of the contributors for their time, their stories and their generosity in collaborating with me on this publication. I would also like to thank Dublin City Council, who commissioned this project through the Per Cent for Art Scheme, for their continued support and commitment to public arts practices that respond to both the everyday and the city.

Chris Reid – December 2010
chrisreidartist.com

1900–19

Patrick Street and Nicholas Street with the steeple of Christchurch Cathedral in the background.

Circa 1900. Photo courtesy of The National Library of Ireland.

Father

A big family and very small means. Me father, William Travers, had a pension from the British Government because he was in the 1914 war. He gave up his job as a sawyer, that's what they called them because he worked on the machines cutting timber and me father had to give up that. He got shrapnel pieces in his face and that little finger was gone. Me mother said 'I'm after seeing Mrs. so and so and she's after being over to the Red Cross and she got blankets and sheets and shoes for her husband and for her young and she after getting any amount of clothes for the bed off the British Legion.' Me father would say, 'I'm not going near any British Legion. I'm not looking for charity I never looked for charity in my life. What I earned I earned.' That's all he had. He took his £1.70.

> "He had a lot of chest trouble. He didn't have it before he went away. He was perfectly healthy and he came back with it. You'd want to hear him coughing. They hadn't him down as being gassed in the war. They say he died from shrapnel in his face and the loss of a little finger." [1]

If we went to get a drink of water at the tap in the backyard and left the tap dripping, he'd shout 'Turn off that tap! I paid ten francs in France for a cup of water!' He was a maniac about the tap; wouldn't let you waste water. He had a lot of chest trouble. He got gassed. He was in the first regiment that the Germans used to gas and they were in the trenches when the first gas was let off. The men didn't know what it was. They weren't prepared for it, no gas masks or nothing. The Germans let off the gas when they were in the trenches. Me father said that when that gas went up it was an awful time. They didn't know how to treat it. They didn't know at all but his chest problem was from the gas. He didn't have it before he went away. He was perfect healthy and he came back with it, the gas got into his chest. He wasn't getting paid for that or for the shrapnel on his face. Little bits of shrapnel, little bits over his face. You could see the little bits on his face but it didn't make any difference to him really. To us he was the very same. He wasn't any

---

1. See page 229

British Army barracks on Ship Street - early twentieth century. Photo courtesy of The National Library of Ireland.

1900–1930

Two soldiers. "In the photo, the man sitting down is my grandfather James Farrell. The man standing up is his brother Willie Farrell." John Freer. Photo courtesy of the Freer family.

different to us. When me father died, the British Government said that we were not entitled to the pension over his disability. No. So they cut me mother off the pension. Me father was fifty-two years of age. He was very young. I was twelve year old when me father died. Me eldest brother was Christy. He was a genius. He was very well educated. He educated himself. He was brilliant. He was good for reading. He could argue with anybody but when he heard me mother was cut off the pension he said, 'That's not right. Me father should have got the pension. You should have got that pension. You're entitled to it.' He went to the library and got books on the war and the Irish regiment and he read them all up and met the priest called Father Browne that me father told them was travelling with them when the gas was let off. The British Government hadn't even got my father down as being gassed in the war. They said he died from the loss of his finger and the shrapnel in his face. But me brother he wrote it all down, everything, and sent it all away to the British Legion and they brought me mother in front of a tribunal. Twelve men sitting around with the red carpet. A tribunal, big chaps, British Army. Me Mam said it's all true. We'd gone through his medical history. None of this was ever recorded but it is true because the hospital is there. She said, 'That's right we looked it up.' He was taken to a hospital with the gas but the British Government they never recorded it. They said, 'Your husband was either a very honest or a very ignorant man.' He should have had a full pension. He died with a chest complaint and it was the gas that did it. So for seven weeks me mother was waiting for a pension while me brother was fighting it, but he recorded everything wrote down on a big foolscap page. He wrote it all down and sent it away and me mother was called to a tribunal to meet these twelve men. Men of the army. 'Your son is very, very intelligent and we've gone through everything he wrote and everything is true. It was never recorded in your husband's history. He had served in the trenches and the priest was with them and that regiment was the first regiment to get the gas. It's all recorded and your husband was in that.' So they said to me mother, 'I only have to say we're only sorry that your husband didn't look for more pension.' He should have been on £4 a week not £1.70. He was very innocent. He was afraid they'd take that off him.

With his chest he couldn't work. You wouldn't want to hear him when he was coughing, 'Oh dear God. Oh God would you never take me.' He'd call for bottle water. Coloured water. Put a bit of powder in the end and shake it all up. That's what was given him for a cough bottle. But it was doing him no good. That's all me father ever got. Me father died in 1943 at 52. Me and me brothers guaranteed to look after me mother.

Letters From France

My granduncle, Owen Brady worked in the British Army. In 1917 he was on manoeuvres and sent this little card to my grandmother, his sister, her name was Margaret Conlan. She lived in No. 59 Bride Street in Dublin. Through this little card, Owen was given options on what he could say to Margaret, he was allowed to delete the sentences that did not fit his situation. The only sentence he did not delete was, 'I am quite well, letter follows at first opportunity'.

Owen was a private in the army and he had a brother called Edward Brady, also in the army. Both Owen and Edward wrote to their sister Margaret on a very regular basis. They would write looking for the shamrock to be sent over to them for Saint Patrick's Day. In other letters Edward would say that he's going to try and get a pair of boots to bring home for my grandfather John Conlan. The military boots were good quality and suitable for my grandfather going to work. When my granduncles would write to their sister – one of the expressions they used was, 'hope this letter finds you as it leaves me – in the pink'. That meant they were in good health and that they were in the pink rather than being pale and drawn.

Both brothers went to the First World War and only one returned. Edward died on duty.

My grandmother Margaret Conlan had ten children, five boys and five girls and my mother, Brigid, was the youngest girl. Owen was the youngest boy in the family. My mother always wanted to know what happened with her uncle Eddie who went missing in the First World War. A couple of year ago, through the internet I found that he had died on the 20th September 1914 and is commemorated in the Commonwealth Graves War Commission in Paris. It's my intention some day to go and stand at that monument and think of him.

A letter sent by Owen Brady to his sister Margaret while on active service during the first world war. Image courtesy of Aileen Morrissey.

.... 1900–1930

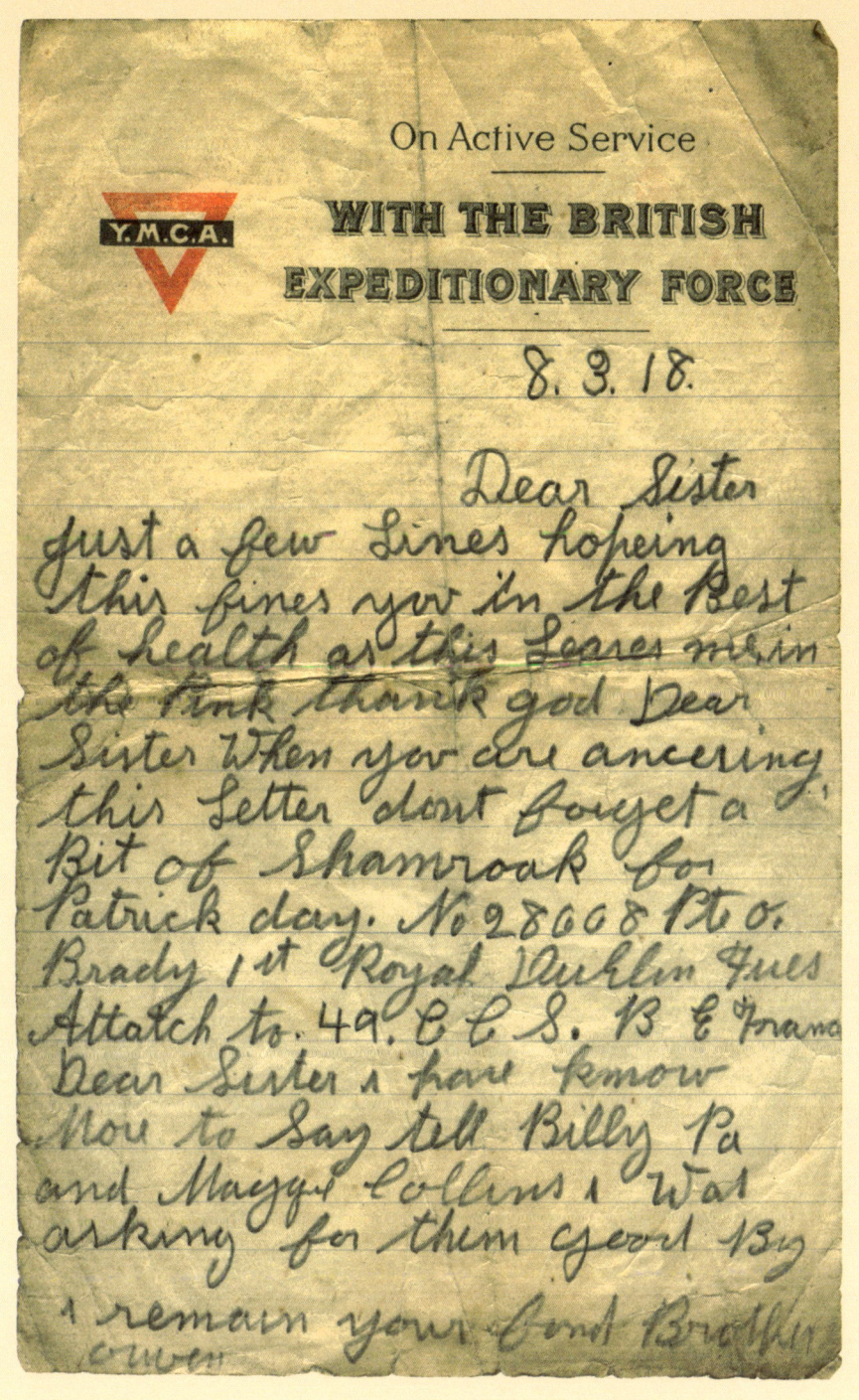

3/158 Union

My grandfather, John Conlan worked in Jacob's biscuit factory at this time and he was a carpenter by trade. He made cabinets, the wooden chests that were used for exporting biscuits. In one of the letters from my granduncles away in 1913 reference is made to the fact that Johnny, got into "a bit of trouble". Now the story in the family is that the "bit of trouble" that my grandfather got into was that during the 1913 Lockout he and some other strikers dumped flour, the property of Jacob's into the Liffey. Also he had unceremoniously delivered one of his ex-coworkers into one of the fountains in St. Patrick's Park. Emotions were running high at the time and he was out on strike and this person had gone back into work. My grandfather, who had mouths to feed as well and he would have liked to have gone back to work but he stuck together with the strikers to win what was needed to be won, during the Lockout.

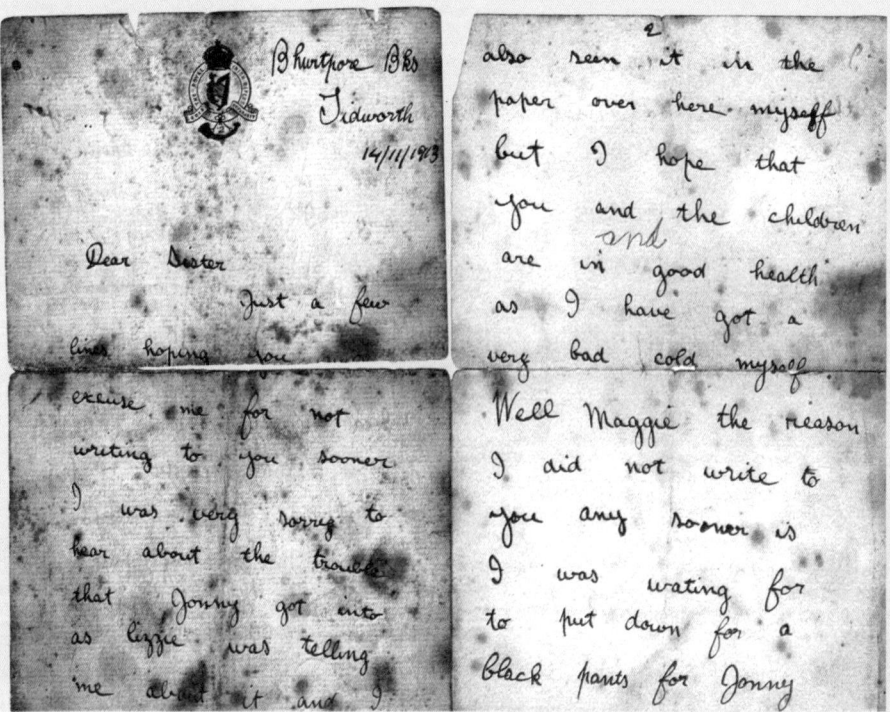

Letter from a granduncle with the British Army that mentions John Conlan's activities as reported in English newspapers during the 1913 Lockout in Dublin. Image courtesy of Aileen Morrissey.

1900–1930

In two of the letters my granduncle wrote that he had heard about the trouble that my grandfather had got into, for throwing the flour into the Liffey and for throwing this man into the pond in St. Patrick's Park. I don't know what happened to the end of that story. This other man was a neighbour who lived nearby and my grandfather knew that he had passed the picket and wasn't too happy with him so I don't know if he ever seen him again. In one of the letters that came from Edward he says 'I've also seen it in the paper over here myself'. There must have been a paragraph or something about it in some of the English papers.

That story has been handed down through the family. My mother was always reared with very strong principles about your entitlements in work and fighting for your rights. She would say that most of the people working in Jacob's knew their rights. And knew their entitlements and would fight for their holidays and make sure that they got their correct pay and all. I think the principles came from her father; her father had a great understanding of workers' rights and entitlements. My father was also very strong in rights for an individual – I had two disabled brothers; Bernard, one brother has Down syndrome. And my older brother John, older than Bernard, got meningitis at seven and he was left disabled. My parents would have had to fight for everything for both of them. My father, Jimmy Wright, was a shop steward with the ITGWU in the Irish Independent newspaper. He was also from Bride Street. As a child I remember that he was involved in one very long strike, I don't know what age I was, all I can remember is I didn't get a present for my birthday that July because my dad was on strike. It could have been about 1964 or thereabouts. You'd often hear about the disputes happening or he'd be in trying to sort problems out.

I am a trade union official myself, obviously there's this bit of militancy in my blood. My grandfather's name was John Conlan and he was Margaret Conlan's husband. Edward Brady and Owen Brady were Margaret's brothers who went to the First World War. So that was my mother's side of the family.

$\frac{4}{158}$ Rebels

My mother's father he was a printer, a compositor in the Irish papers at the time. They broke his fingers; he was printing one of the illegal newspapers at the time too. I don't know what the name of the paper was but later he was working for the Irish Press.

25

Christopher Halpin. He was one of the four buglers at the raising of the flag at Liberty Hall, 1916. He was from Nicholas Street. He was only a kid around that time of the Rising. Sixteen or something. He wasn't involved, he was the bugler. Done it a couple of times a week. He was in that place on Church Street; he was in the Boys' Brigade, something like that. They'd practice in a hall there in Church Street there, march through Saint Audoen's Church, which is across the road from where we were in Nicholas Street. Years later he was also in the Naval Reserve. He moved to Old Cabra and lived to over a hundred.

$\frac{5}{158}$ Grandmother

It was my Gran's mum, Marcella Curran, who originally moved onto Bride Street when my Gran, Eileen Curran, was 14, that would have been 1915. They lived in 2B Bride Street. Gran had two children Eileen and Patrick Curran. My mum recalls her mum telling her that during the 1916 Uprising, they would have to lay down in the flats as gun shots were being fired down Bride Street from Dublin Castle.

Four years after moving into 2B Bride Street Eileen Curran married William Wright from the Iveagh Flats. William Wright is my grandfather and married my Gran in 1919. He was in the British Army. My mum is assuming they met in the neighborhood but does remember going in the Iveagh Flats to visit the grandparents, William and Margaret Wright. My mother was born in 1922 and lived in 2B Bride Street. Later they did move from 2B to 4A and then again to 4D (on the 2nd floor). This is where my Gran remained until 1962.

My Gran was a single mother. Her husband left her with 3 small children. My Gran, Eileen Wright, lived and raised her children (William, Agnes and James) in the flats on Bride Street. Twice a day, my Gran would head to Dublin Castle where her job was to light the fires and clean out the fireplaces. She would leave the house around 4:00am and go back in the evenings from 5:00pm to 7:00pm to clean out the fireplaces. During this time, Dublin Castle was Government Offices. Being a single mother, and having no child care, she would lock the children in the apartment and head to work. In the morning the children would have to feed and dress themselves to get ready for school. They would go to school when she returned. As my mother, Agnes, who is today eighty-nine, headed to Basin Street school she remembered meeting up with her own grandmother who would be coming home from working at

.... 1900–1930

Eileen Wright with her children, Agnes, William and James. Circa 1920s. Eileen Wright lived in Bride Street from 1915 to 1962. Photo courtesy of Siobhan VanDeKeere.

the Guinness factory (the majority of my Gran's family including my uncle Bill Wright worked in Guinness's). My mother with her brothers remembers sliding down the pipes after her mother left for work to play with the children in the street and climbing back up before her mother got home.

As we grew up, we asked Gran about her husband, she would tell us that he was killed in the war, or was in a train accident. We have now learnt that he actually left her because he had another family out of the country, where he was with the army. We don't know many details, but obviously it was painful for my Gran to talk about. I am not sure where they lived after they got married but she moved back in with her mother when her husband left her.

My mother married Johnny Byrne. They moved out to Bray after they were married, where my father took over his uncle's tailor store. In 1957 my father emigrated to Canada, my mother moved back in with her mother in 4D Bride Street, with 6 children under the age of 12. My sisters, Fran & Doreen, recall living on Bride Street in 1957 (they were 7 & 9) and being very much the outcasts. Since my father was a tailor, the children were very well dressed and they were country girls from Bray! They looked like they had money, but really didn't. They were quickly taken care of by a group of girls from the neighbourhood, who made sure no one messed with the country girls. They attended Francis Street School & Basin Lane School.

A year later my mother and the family moved to Inchicore. They lived there for a year until my father sent for them to join him in Winnipeg, Canada in 1959. In 1962 they brought my Gran to Winnipeg where she lived with us till her passing in October 1994, just a month short of her 93rd birthday. I was born and raised in Canada, but was in Dublin last year for a visit. I still have family in Dublin, on my father's and mother's side but none live in the Bride Street area now.

My sister Fran had also visited it in 2008 with my cousin Aileen who lives in Dublin. They were taking a photograph of the apartment building and a lady came out of 4A to say hello to them and was wondering why they were taking a photograph of the building. She brought Aileen and Fran in to have a look at the flat now but they didn't recall the lady's name.

The picture (page 27) shows my Gran with my mum and my two uncles when they would've been living on Bride Street around 1926.

.... 1900–1930

$\frac{6}{158}$ Mark of a Bullet

Me father was in the First World War, when he came home like he was a bit delicate; he wasn't able to work like, you know, as a result of the war. Yea, they came home with war wounds and things like that, you know, so he never worked; me mother always worked. He died of TB. During the war, I think he was shot or something. I often heard me brothers saying it, that he was shot in the forehead or that, you know, because he had the mark of a bullet in his forehead. That time the men got nothing like, you know, when they came home from the First World War there was nothing really, they got nothing, no pensions or anything like that. So me mother then went out to work, me mother always worked, because when we were kids we had to come in and get our own meals ready, and get our stuff ready for the next morning for school. They nearly all had somebody belonging to them killed in the war, like me mother had, I think, a brother killed in the Battle of the Somme, and me father had a brother killed in the First World War, so really like, everyone had someone belonging to them, going back in them days.

$\frac{7}{158}$ The Suitcase

I found a suitcase under her bed. I couldn't believe it, all the papers I was pulling out, you know. She kept everything relating to that time. I mean she had papers from the Civil War, you know, little news sheets I guess they were called. Seven or eight of those. But she kept all that stuff. I took them out and sorted them out and then brought them home, got the family together and showed them all to the family. They couldn't believe it either. And all the papers, everything. There's about thirty or forty pieces of paper and all the little things from Bridie's jail journal that she got from all the different girls that were in there (see page 160). All little things in there. And you know I was holding that thing in my hand, that book that was so... the little pages were sewn together, it just blew my mind you know. Sewn together, little pieces of paper in prison. I guess you could get paper in that place at that time. And correspondence from Maud Gonne McBride. She never even mentioned things like this (see page 32).

1900–1930 ....

8/158 Civil War

I have no idea when Bridie Halpin joined Cumann na mBan, no idea. She would have been, she was only eighteen I believe when she was in prison so I'm sure it was within two years of that. She only would have been twelve or thirteen then during the Rising so she would have been too young to take part. I've no idea what she did in Cumann na mBan or what rank she was.

I wouldn't say she was high up because she was too young at the time. Bridie was involved in the Irish Civil War; that's why she was in prison I guess. She was in prison during the Civil War. We never found out what for. She never spoke about it, nobody spoke about it after that generation. That was it, it was an unknown, people didn't talk about it. I think it was more or less the shame of it being that Bridie was on the losing side, it wasn't talked about. Her name and her address were scrawled on the wall in that cell that I saw but also, and I think this was over the door of that cell, I can't remember, but there was a great little passage she had written. It says – 'far better the grave of a rebel without cross, without stone, without name than a treaty with treacherous England that can only bring sorrow and shame.' Bridie Halpin, Kilmainham Gaol (see page 169). Such a powerful pen and a powerful phrase from this meek little woman. I mean she had to be four foot nine or four foot ten; a tiny woman you know.

Bridie went to New York; she went in '48. She worked at a Hotel Pierre, the Pierre. For probably about thirty years. I don't think she missed Nicholas Street. She used to talk about the times she used to go down the country for a holiday, you know. And she used to have a good time but they lost their parents at a very early age too. So they more or less raised themselves. There

Bridie Halpin's name and address, No. 4 Nicholas Street, were written in pencil on the wall of a cell in Kilmainham Gaol. Photo courtesy of Kilmainham Gaol Museum.

1900–1930

Portrait of Bridie Halpin 1920s. Photo courtesy of Christopher Halpin & the Kilmainham Gaol Museum.

was her oldest brother Christopher and then Bridie was next and then May and my father, and then the youngest. They were the five children. My father, he was the fourth.

> can no longer get round. thats all the news from Roebuck.
> I expect you will be home on a holiday some time & we all shall be so happy to see you. Next time you write tell me about yourself — I hope you are happy, & enjoying life. Best of luck to you & God bless you —
> Your old friend
> Maud Gonne MacBride
>
> Roebuck House
> Clonskea —
> Co Dublin.
> 25th Nov. 47
> It was so nice of you to write & tell me you liked my articles in the Irish World. Thank you —

Page of a letter written by Maud Gonne McBride and sent to Bridie Halpin. Image courtesy of Christopher Halpin and The Kilmainham Gaol Museum.

9/158 Holes in His Legs

My father's name was John Donnelly. I never used to believe me mother when she'd say, 'Sure he has holes in his legs from the bullets.' Like they must have known at the time, what happened to him, because he was found in a trench, you know, he was lying there for days before he was found. Well me mother, Elizabeth Donnelly, heard it from his sister, my Aunt Katie. She used to tell us all the stories, but he wouldn't. In fact she gave me a badge. It's an old army badge that me father wore, must have been from his cap or his clothes, and she had a spoon belonging to him and everything, and she used to be telling us, like me father was days in this trench when he was found, and this is how he had the holes, he couldn't walk you see, after this happened to him, that's how he just had to lie there, and sure there used to be rats and everything in those trenches, and all the dead all lying around him, you know.

When he came out of the army, this country was poverty stricken, there was no work whatsoever, but because he was in the British Army, and of course

A group of men serving in the British Army during the 1st World War. John Donnelly is in the first row and second from the left. Photo courtesy of Harriet Donnelly.

1900–1930

the British were here, he got a job in the Post Office. He was in it all his life, until he died. He got it through the Army. He always went to bed early as he'd be up at four o'clock in the morning. In the bedroom where me father slept we had a table, and we used to have our meals there, and the fire would be going. In the evening we had our dinner or tea and then we all left. Me father could then get some sleep. One evening I happened to go back into the room, and me father, I didn't realise, being so young, I suppose, that he was getting ready for bed. He was sitting on the bed you see, and he hadn't taken his clothes off or anything, he pulled up his trousers and he had these white long johns as they called them then, they used to keep him warm in the winter, and he just happened to pull one leg, and I just remember seeing these holes, and I knew

.... 1900–1930

then me mother was telling the truth. And later I told me mother, 'I saw the holes', says she, 'Yea, of course,' you know. Some of them you could nearly put your finger into them. I couldn't believe it now... I never asked me father about them. You didn't ask your father questions like that. Me mother said he had medals, but me mother said, 'You should have kept them.' She was always on about these medals. What did he do when he left the army – he pawned them, and never redeemed them (see plaque 3 on page 71). He died sixty-four, with cancer of the lungs, 1957.

Queues for food on Castle Street 1922. Photo courtesy of The National Library of Ireland.

1900–1930

10/158 Moving House

My father, John Freer, died long before I moved into Bride Street when I was twelve year old. The father was in the First World War, and the reason he was in the First World War was to bring in the wages to keep the family; no work, and strikes all that time. And that's how the British Army got so many men out of Ireland. To feed their families they went, those men. Oh he's an Offaly man by God, my father was an Offaly man. The roots is in Tullamore. He told me very, very little about his war time experiences; you couldn't get anything out of him. Never talked about it. Got a pension and all out of it, but never talked about it. I didn't ask him, no, because like I was in the army myself, and by the grace of God we weren't called up, like our country – Ireland – didn't go to war. I was in the Irish Army.

So anyway we moved then to the country when my father got an ex-service house so moved down there. He was an ex-serviceman, he had a pension, he got one of them houses, it was a double house, it was Kelly's on one side and us on this side. And it was up a bothereen, about a mile and a half from the town. But we were there for lots of years, and the father is buried down there. The mother is gone, we got her back up here as well, there's nobody down there now. I don't know whether there's any of the family left or not, I couldn't tell you. That's the way....

My father was very tight-lipped about that. He got wounded and he got gassed. I know he got wounded because I seen the wound, and he got gassed. The proof of that was he got his pension. The British Army didn't give you a pension for nothing. So he wasn't telling lies, what happened did happen, you know what I mean, they wouldn't...the British Army tried to avoid giving you a pension if they possibly can. His breathing was affected, he was under a doctor for the rest of his life. I often used to be with him at the doctor, there used to be Dr. Crowe at Christchurch, Lord Edward Street, that's the one. There was a bedding place there – Richardson's, and overhead used to be the doctors.

Aunt Nellie and Grandparents Helen and John Redmond, No. 3 Bride Street, 1927. Photo courtesy of Fergus Redmond.

19

Wally and Nora's wedding 1934. Photo taken in the yard at the back of the flats on Bride Street. Photo courtesy of Fergus Redmond.

30s

1930s ....

11/158 Eucharistic Congress

1932, I was up in the Park with my father, God be good to him. I was, how old was I that time, ah it was up in the 15 acres, I think they called it, in the Park, they had a big altar built out in the wide open space you know, thousands of people around. I remember that very, very well. I was living in 39 South Earl Street, off Meath Street, at that time. People decorated the street, very much so, but like you could hardly get into the Park it was that packed. It's a big place to pack. I remember that very well, although I was only a toddler as I said, I must have been what, what year was that – 1932. Twelve year old so I was.

Only the two of us was up. Being a child that doesn't really sort of move you, you are going down, somebody has you by the hand bringing you around it's… you know, kids they are looking around, that's… I wasn't much interested in the… I didn't care who he was, at that time, you know, I was a kid. No use in saying he's this, that or the other, I hadn't a clue. A child at twelve year old and what, I bet you you'd be the same as I was. You would have been, I know you would have been. Like as a child that age all you are interested in is your own bits and pieces.

Processions

We went to the Whitefriar Street School, and every third Sunday there was a procession, first of all in the church, and even before I made me First Communion my mother had to buy me a white dress, for to walk in this procession, because me sister was walking, and I wanted to walk, of course. So she bought me a white dress, and somebody lent me a veil, and the little wreath to go on me head, so I used to walk in the procession. My father and all the other confraternity men, they had the Carmelite habits, and they'd put them on, the big brown scapular you know, and my father would be at the head of the procession, holding the banner with another man, and they'd lead the procession, and we'd all walk around the church, keep walking around, and walking around. And then the Corpus Christi procession was from Meath Street, and we used to walk all round the area. The priest would come first, carrying the Blessed Sacrament all around here, the people used to decorate their windows.

The procession could go down various streets. If it was John's Lane, or if it was Meath Street, or Francis Street, you went up Thomas Street, around into Meath Street, down around Carman Hall, you came back down Carman Hall, back down into Francis Street, the church is there, and you turned right at the church again, and you went down there into Ardee Street, around into Patrick Street, and then you went up the Bull Road, and now this was years ago, they shortened it as the years went on. Came down here, all around. Turn down this way to Bride Street. sometimes they'd go up the Ross Road, or go up around Christchurch, back around into Francis Street, you know. All the people, we used all have the windows decorated with pictures of the Sacred Heart and Our Lady and all, everyone used to put something in their window because the procession would be going by, you know, the bunting used be up along the windows and all, and then all different colours, there was red,

People kneel and pray at the Eucharistic Congress in The Phoenix Park, 1932. Photo courtesy of The National Library of Ireland.

1930s

and there was white, and there was yellow, and there was green. We used to buy the material and cut it up, and if you knew someone to stitch them all into a big long thing, you know. Some people would have them from the year before; you'd keep it you see, to the next year, everyone was always prepared for things like that.

Whitefriar Street Confraternity. John Donnelly – centre of the 1st row. Photo courtesy of Harriet Donnelly.

Yard at the back of Bride Street. From right to left, Elizabeth Donnelly, Mrs. Sheridan, Annie Lyons. Photo courtesy of Harriet Donnelly.

13/158 First Communion

My First Holy Communion. Oh God I'll never forget it. A wonderful time. Had a dress like a princess and a cape and bonnet. Oh it was wonderful. My mother got it made specially because she had five boys and I was the first girl so I needn't tell you me mother thought nothing too good for me.

It was mostly wreathes and veils. I had a bonnet made for me by Kellets on George's Street, where Dunnes is now. It used to be a big drapery shop – a lovely big drapery upstairs and downstairs. It sold materials and suits.

The dress was satin and there was Irish lace over it. That was the fashion people went in for. Me mother went overboard, me being her first girl making her Communion after having five boys. You never forget your Communion. I remember when they used to have the first Sunday in May. We had the processions and you wore your Communion dress. I'm eighty-one now. I must have been seven making my Communion. It must have been the late 1930s. I was only about 7. You made your Communion at seven and your Confirmation at ten. Catechism you had to learn a lot. I remember I did my Confirmation when I was eleven, and I had to learn a lot of stuff from my catechism like 'Who is God?' and 'Who is the divine person?' I had to learn about the Blessed Sacrament. We had to learn all these prayers. They were difficult but they weren't too hard. We learnt them in the school and we used to learn the prayers at home. We used to say our prayers at home and sing the prayers.

Before my Confirmation I was put at the end of the seat. I was put there on purpose if the bishop was there to ask questions. He didn't; I was very disappointed. He asked others what does Confirmation mean to you but he didn't ask me anything, just skipped and went to the next row. I was disgusted. People were very innocent in those times.

14/158 Play

I was at the Meath Street School. There was a derelict house in front of ours, a big derelict space where we used to play. Now it wasn't Cowboys and Indians now, we used to play bang-bang war because the Great War was after being over shortly and we used to kill all the Germans all around the place, there wouldn't be a German left alive, all this carry on. Then we used to have a

1930s

1938 Graffiti on the gable wall of the Iveagh Trust Flats on Bull Alley. Photo courtesy of Chris Reid.

Billy can and we used to boil it with water and make what we'd call tea for ourselves and all that carry on, only kids now, you know what I mean, only twelve year old. And my arm went into the boiling water. I got a scalded arm, so I hopped, I didn't say anything to anybody, I just went out and in the big yard there was a big community hall in the back and I went there and put my arm under the tap. It's supposed to be the best thing I could have done, but I didn't know at the time. All I wanted was to get the fuzzy feeling out of my arm. And my mother, Mary Freer, called me the next morning and she nearly had a fit. There was blisters that size on my arm, all over the one arm. I had to get off school every morning to go up to the hospital to get my arm dressed. Up to the Meath hospital and get my arm dressed. And maybe I'd be an hour there and then I'd be back to school. But then I started extending my time, instead of it being an hour, used to be two hours, eventually I used to be out kicking football in Harold's Cross Park and I started mitching from school.

15/158 What Your Mother Said Was Law

You see they spoke even in front of children as if you weren't there, sort of thing, but yet if they were talking about anything, anything that wasn't nice, you had to get out of the way, you know, because I often was out with my mother and she'd be going up the markets for to buy her vegetables, and going for her meat for the dinner, and she'd meet someone, and they'd start talking about, you know, babies and all that, and she used say, 'You go on over there, you can't hear this,' you know, 'You're not supposed to hear this.' So you were never let hear things that you shouldn't, that they felt would do you harm, or fill your mind with the wrong thoughts or anything, you know, everything is so different today – you couldn't answer your mother back, you know the way they say things to their parents now – I do be amazed, because if my mother said anything to anyone, and you went to answer back, she'd say, 'What did you say?' 'Sorry Ma.' You know, 'I didn't mean it, it just slipped out.' Because I think you felt your parents knew better than you did, which was true, they did, they had lived through life. We sort of knew instinctively that your father and your mother knew what they were talking about, this is how we were taught.

"Those days were all so innocent. You weren't afraid to go down the street, or go anywhere or talk to anyone. We were let stay out to about eight o'clock. My mother wouldn't even let us stay in the house, because if we came up here she'd say 'What's wrong with you? Are you sick? Why are you not out playing? She wouldn't allow us to stay in all day especially if the weather was good. She'd say, 'Go out and enjoy God's sunshine.'" [2]

2. See page 229

1930s

Always the little story they told you, to get the message across. There was a child one time, and he used answer back his parents, and something happened to him, and he died, and you know when they buried him, his hand came up through the grave, his hand was up like that in the grave, because he raised his hand to his mother, and he used to answer them back, he was cheeky, you know.

16/158 We Didn't Have Locks

Everyone knew everyone else here. You could hear the people going up and down the stairs, you know, at one stage when we were very young, we put the front door 'on the lock' a hole bored into the door, a piece of twine tied around it, through the twine was put through it, so that like as kids and all, we were up and down all the time, anybody that came up just had to pull the string, and all the tenants had this.

> "There were no locks on the doors as such. A hole was bored into the door and a piece of twine was put through it." [3]

You know you could walk into anyone's home, but nobody did because, you know, we respected other people's homes, but you wouldn't walk in. But you could do it like, if you were that way inclined, but no one did, because nobody, we hadn't anything really to take on them, you know, and everybody was the same way, we were all just barely getting by. I mean my father worked in the Post Office, but the wages wasn't good then. At one stage I think he was earning six pound a week, and there was six of us to be kept for a week, you know, but we always had enough.

3. See page 229

Childhood Illness

I must have been about ten, I can't remember rightly, but I remember crossing the road, and everything suddenly went black, and I must have been crying or screaming or something, but Mrs. Sheridan, Lord have mercy on her, lived underneath, and she was looking out the front window, and I heard her voice saying, 'What's wrong with you love' and I was delighted to hear her voice, and next thing I heard her speaking to someone, and I recognised me mother's voice, so the two of them came over, and me mother said, 'Come on, I'll get you up to bed'.

"We respected other people's homes. You could walk into anyone's home, if you were that way inclined, but no one did. Anyway we hadn't anything worth taking. Everyone was the same way, we were all barely getting by." [4]

I was weeks in bed, I don't know what was wrong, I said to my sister Kathleen, 'What was wrong with me then?'. She said it was gastritis, as they called it, now I don't know what it was, but I used to have terrible nightmares and all, and my mother didn't believe in doctors, you know. She wouldn't get a doctor for you, she used say, 'I'll cure you meself,' she used to say, all the mothers did. They couldn't afford to pay them, you know, and all the mothers were the same, they all had these old fashioned remedies. 'I'll cure you meself'' she used to say, so I don't know what she was giving me, but I was lying in the bed, and the next thing, this particular day, John Donnelly my brother, he was fourteen, the eldest, he had got his first job, and it was his first week's wages, and I'll always remember. I was lying in the bedroom there, and me mother and father, they were all out here in the other room, and next thing he came into the bedroom with his hands behind his back, and he said to me, 'Guess what I have for you'? And I looked up and said, 'I don't know. 'Ah guess', he kept saying to me, and I said, 'I can't, I don't know'. So with that, he brought his hands around, and there was a black doll, I always remember it, dressed and all, and it had the hat on it, and I was over the moon over this. You know we didn't get many toys

4. See page 229

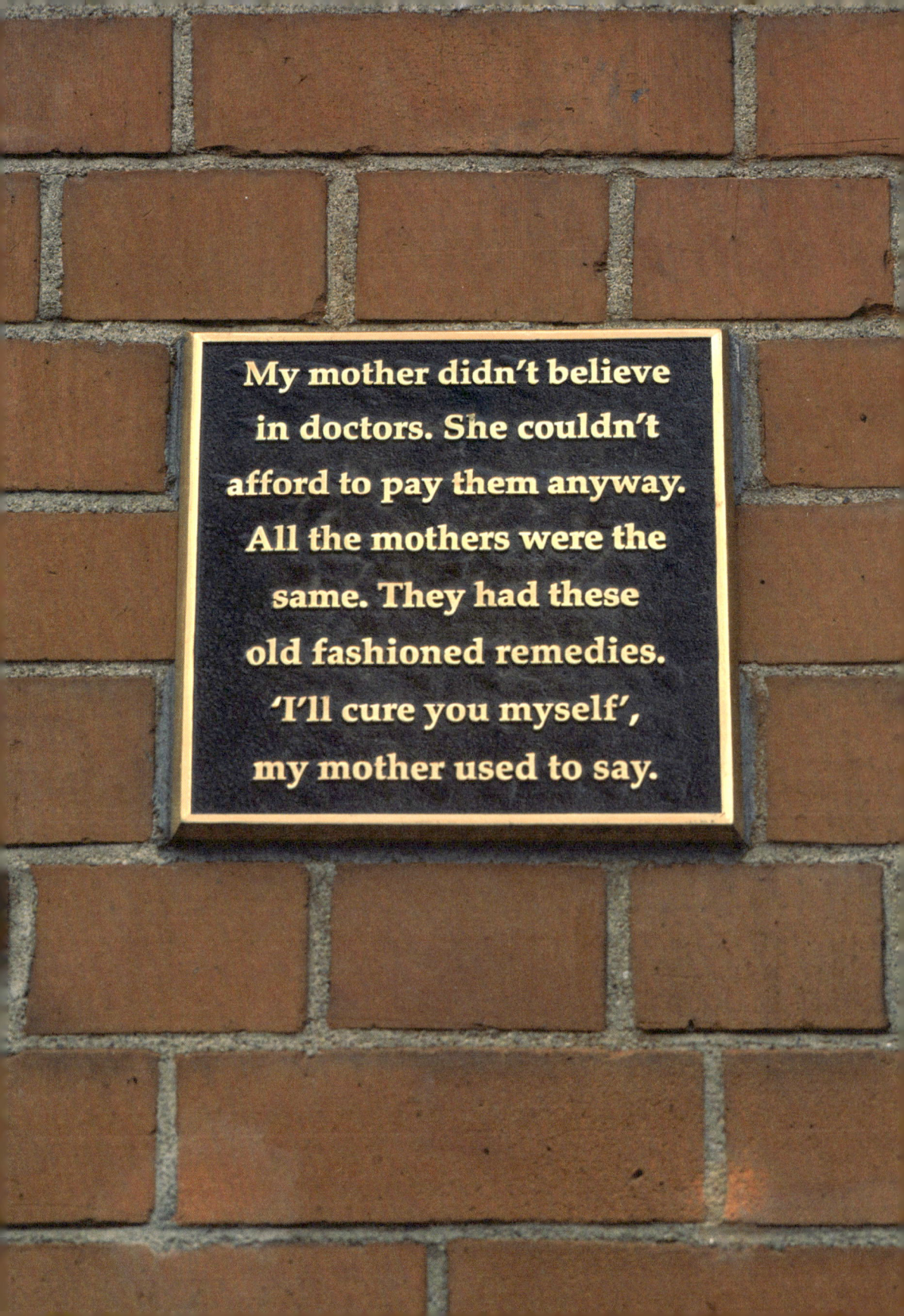

My mother didn't believe in doctors. She couldn't afford to pay them anyway. All the mothers were the same. They had these old fashioned remedies. 'I'll cure you myself', my mother used to say.

then, because you were lucky if you got one toy at Christmas. I never forgot him for that, because it was his first week's wages, his first job, and here he was, he had spent his pocket money on this doll, you know.

18/158 Getting a Job

One day I heard my mother and my father talking, I heard something about John going away, and being so young I didn't understand, and I didn't ask questions about it. He was only seventeen then and he wanted to get a job. He went up to the Labour Exchange in Werburgh Street, and they said, 'We've no jobs' and he said 'Well what am I supposed to live on?' 'You can join the army, the Irish Army,' they said and John nearly went mad, and he said, 'Look I want a proper job.' 'You'll be in the Irish Army,' they said to him. 'I don't want to be in the Irish Army,' he said, 'I want a job that I can earn a proper week's wages. I see them – the Irish Army,' he said, 'coming home at lunch time on their bikes,' he said. They insisted, and gave him papers to fill in, so he tore them up in front of them. He didn't want to go away, and leave, you know, but all the lads like around his age, they used to be all on the corner here. He said to me, 'Look I'm not going to spend years standing on the corner, like the rest of them I see around the area.' So he came back, and early one morning he got up and went up to the North. When he came back he told me mother he was after joining the British Army. He found out all what he needed to know before he went. He knew he wouldn't be taken until he was eighteen, but because he was only gone seventeen, he changed his birth certificate to eighteen and he was taken on.

19/158 They Passed Remarks

When John came home on leave, he used to come down in his civilian clothes and he used be lovely. In fact Kathleen, his sister, used to say to him, 'Why did you have to be my brother?' because he was good looking then. He was young and all, and he was spotless, because being in the army you had to be immaculate, you know. He had a beautiful navy crombie coat on him. I remember, he came home one particular time, before he was shipped out and when he was still based in England, and he was walking down the street one day, and all the lads was at the corner when he'd walk by.

Bronze plaque installed on Bride Street 2008. Story no. 17/158. See no. 20 on page 8 and 9.
Photo by Chris Reid.

Werburgh Street, Dublin. Early twentieth century. Photo courtesy of The National Library of Ireland.

"The lads at the corner jeered at him when he passed. They were still idle, had no jobs and he was in the army. The British Army." [5]

They were still idle, got no jobs, and he was in the Army, you know, awaiting to be shipped overseas and they always passed remarks when he passed. This time they were all giving out to him, jeering him and everything. I don't know quite what they said, he never told us, but me sister used to hear them, and she gave out to them, she eat the head off them all, she was gas, Kathleen, you know. But she came running up to the flat, and John had come up, and she said to him, 'Why do you let them say them things to you?' And me mother, who was there too, says, 'What things?' 'They're jeering him because he's in the British Army, and saying things,' you know. And John says 'I wouldn't be bothered, I wouldn't lower meself to answer them, what do you want me to do?' he said, 'I'd rather be the way I am, than be like them, standing holding up the corner all day,' he said, you know, 'at least I'm earning a living, OK, I'm in England, and I'm getting the Queen's shilling,' as he said, 'but I don't care, my self-respect is more important, and I don't care who gives it to me, as I'm doing an honest day's work, and I'm getting an honest week's pay, that's all that worries me.' But it was in him too, you see, with me father being in the British Army as well, you know.

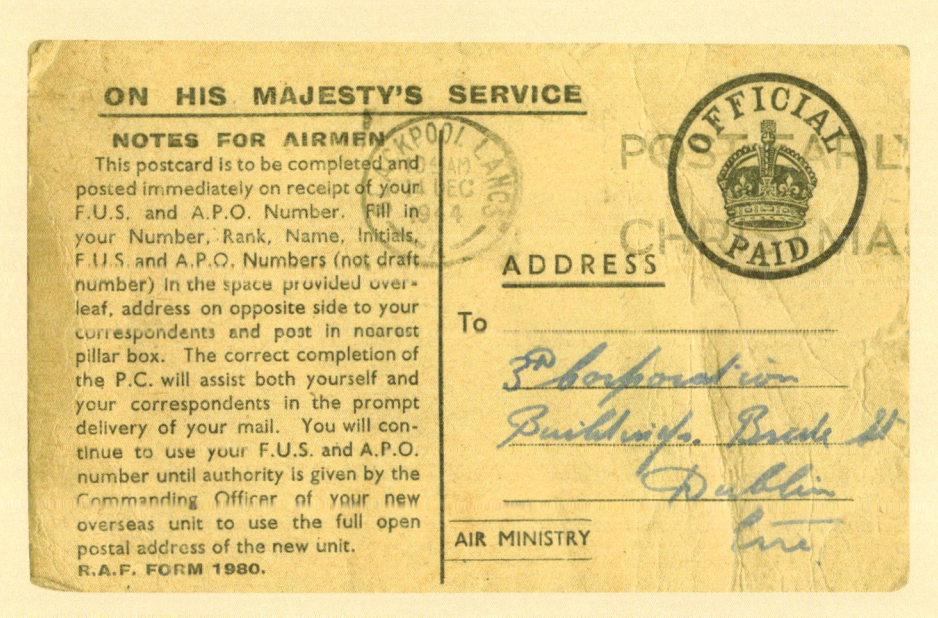

British Army postcard sent home by John Donnelly. Courtesy of Harriet Donnelly.

5. See page 229

19

40s

View of Nicholas Street from Patrick Street. All the buildings on the left have since been demolished and the road widened by over twice the width shown in this image. Photo courtesy of Steven Freer.

20/158 Faith of Our Fathers, and Mothers

Me father was quite religious, me mother was very religious, going out, she would have got her Mass every day, and me father, the Lord be good to him, made sure that we got our Mass on a Sunday, especially after making our First Communion, he'd have us at Mass, at ten o'clock on Sunday morning. He loved Clarendon Street Church; he was very devout at Clarendon Street. And I'd see me mother, before she'd get Communion in the mornings, she'd wash her feet. She'd have a basin of water washing her feet, before she'd receive the Communion. And that time they fasted overnight before going over to make their Communion, they didn't get their breakfast until they came back, but it's all changed now. They were devout Catholics. We weren't under strict rule or that, you know like, we could do whatever we like, you know, stay out late at night, and I could bring friends up to the house and that.

.... 1940s

The processions – every May were lovely, they were up in Mount Argus. When we made our Communion, we walked in the procession every Sunday, the May procession, for the whole month of May you walked every Sunday in your procession and you wore your Communion dress. Now you see kids now making their Communion – the dresses are all put up there, never wore again. Back then you'd wear it again, you know, No such thing like spending hundreds on a suit, and leaving it lying up there. You'd wear your clothes until they were wore out or it was passed on.

Aerial photograph (1940s) showing from left to right, Fishamble Street, John's Lane East, Lord Edward Street and Christchurch Place. Image courtesy of the Irish Architectural Archive.

1940s

21/158 Sunshine House

The first time that I was able to go to the Sunshine House in Balbriggan was in 1941. One week before you went you had to go and get examined, you know, to see if there was anything in your head or if you had any nits or sores. You went for that before you went. A health check up in Myra Hall.

You went on the train on a Saturday and the following Saturday you came home. The kids would have ranged from about eight to twelve, you know. The boys went one week and the girls the other. You went to get off the train at Balbriggan, you'd get off and the boys would be getting on to go back home. It was a week for the boys and a week for the girls. And you had adult lay people there and you'd call them sisters and brothers, they kind of looked after you. They were, kind of, you know, ordinary people who gave their time as they do now. I remember there was a sister Redmond and she lived, I always remember she lived up there off Rathmines.

It was during the war so you brought your rations with you, you went to Amiens Street Station and got the train to Balbriggan. And then you went to what we called the Sunshine House. There was a dormitory with a lot of beds in it. You got up in the morning and washed in cold water, then you lined up and got your prayer book and you walked up to the town and got Mass. Everyone had to say their prayers. You went to Mass every morning up in the town. You'd come out walk up from it and up the road. There were thatched cottages all along in the main street where the church is. After Mass you walked back and you came back to Sunshine House and got your breakfast. And then you either went down to the beach and made sandcastles or went in the water. And then you'd go back and get your dinner, or whatever, you'd eat. I can't remember very much about it, it was plain food. You ate it and were glad to get it. And then there was two swings and a slide in the grounds and you'd play on that or play games and get your tea, I can't remember really what you got. But then you had a concert as we called it then and people were asked to sing and people got up to sing. I sang, Twinkle Twinkle Little Star. I was 8, and I got a prize I can't remember what it was at the end of the week. You went to bed at 8 – everyone had to say their prayers. It was great to go, I went I think three times.

22/158 My Father's Voice

My father made sure we went to Mass and he was on the door. If you didn't go like, he would know we weren't there. Every third Sunday they used to have this procession in the church. And he would walk all around and any children who made their First Holy Communion could wear their dress and veil and join the procession. And at the time I wasn't still old enough to make my First Holy Communion and I always remember my mother went out and bought me a dress and it was second hand. And the Iveagh Market was a great place for picking up things like that. And she bought me this dress and it was something that I couldn't wear every day. But because I was going in the procession I insisted, and I was always my father's favourite. But anyway I was in the procession on the Thursday night. My father was always up front and my father had a very deep voice. And when they would be singing the hymns you would hear him all around the church. And in Whitefriar school in one of the classes, you were in the one class all day. But you were taught different subjects. Like the singing hour, when the teacher would be teaching us singing. And then she would call on someone, and of course this particular day she called me. And I started to sing what she had taught us and she stopped me, and said, 'Your voice is too low. Sing out stronger than that.' So I started again and she stopped me again, and she said 'You are still too low.' And I said, 'I can't sing any louder.' 'Well you are not your father's daughter,' she said to me, 'You would hear your father out in the park.'

23/158 Work Inside and Outside The Home

My mother was a cleaner, and then she was the cook in Dublin Castle, she done all the cooking there for the detectives and that, and she worked in Kevin Street Barracks. I'd say it would have been going into the 40s she worked in Kevin Street Barracks. She done the cooking up there too. She was always hard working and that, you know. She done all our washing over in the wash house, you know, there was a laundry there beside the Iveagh Market, and she'd go over there, and for sixpence she got three hours, be able to do all the washing there, and that was by hand. Speed was the name of the washing powder, a little shop in Francis Street, you'd run over and get a packet of powder, or maybe black soap, we called the black soap "dirt shifter".

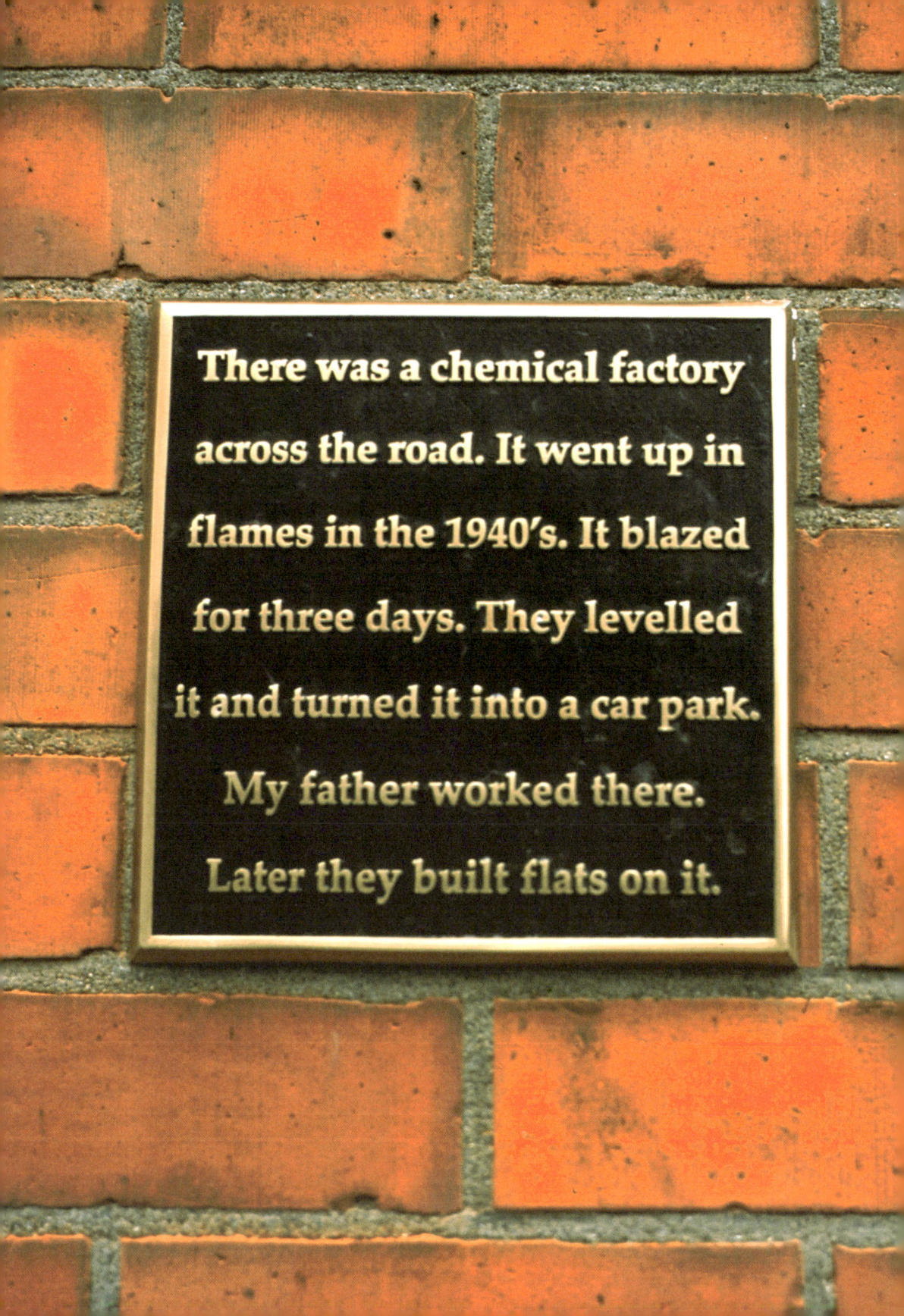

There was a chemical factory across the road. It went up in flames in the 1940's. It blazed for three days. They levelled it and turned it into a car park. My father worked there. Later they built flats on it.

.... 1940s

We'd have a washing board then scrubbing the clothes and that, you know. Washing machines only lasted a year or two, I'd say, the washing board never breaks. Yea, they were very hard workers and that, you know.

The market? The Iveagh owned that, they sold it over to the Corporation, and the Corporation then like they run it then, people used have stalls and that. We were always over there when we were children, looking at them selling all the clothes and that. There was a woman had a shop in Bride Street, and her sister sold clothes in the market, Chrissie Young and I, she'd give us a mug, a canister of tea to bring up to her, and her sandwiches, we used to love going over to the market, giving her her tea and her sandwiches, you know, we used to like going all round the stalls, looking at them selling all the second-hand clothes and that, and it was something to do on a Saturday morning.

$\frac{24}{158}$ Quaker Style Care For Workers

My mother Bridget Conlan like her father worked in Jacob's. Her sister Mary worked in the cake making section in Jacob's factory and the brother Pat also worked there. People nowadays just know Jacob's for biscuits but they did cakes as well. Jacob's was a big employer and then so was Guinness. Jacob's had a Quaker like style of looking after their employees, including their medical, housing, with a lot of welfare structures internally within the organization. They would have been good employers in my mother's time. When Mam was a young child they moved to a Jacob's house on Cuffe Lane and they left Bride Street. There was a lottery for Jacob's houses and they got a house through the lottery. They moved around into Cuffe Lane, which is not ten minutes walk from Bride Street, behind Mercer buildings. And I think there's 12 houses or maybe 13 houses there in a small little cul-de-sac done in a little square. At the time it was a great thing to get your house. When you are in a flat with maybe ten children it was great to get a house. They had a front garden and all and a little yard out the back. And that's where they lived then, so they didn't move too far away from Bride Street.

My mother's eldest sister and her husband looked after the Jacob's horses. The stables, I remember as a child in the 60s that the Jacob's horses were stalled in Cuffe Lane. And I remember those horses coming out of there and going around to Jacob's factory in Bishops Street. Just around the corner.

Bronze plaque installed on Bride Street 2008. See no. 10 on page 8 and 9. Photo by Chris Reid.

Net Curtains and White Sheets

We had nets, net curtains, me mother Elizabeth Donnelly, used to take great pride, all the people did, took great pride out of their net curtains, and at that time, as I said, as hard as it was to do the washing, because I was saying to you, me mother had the tin bath, all the people were the same, except for the people that had the big crowd of children, and went up to the wash house, at the side of the Iveagh Market, but my mother used to do all her washing in this big tin bath, and she had the board, the scrubbing board, and after that then she'd take down the nets, and she'd wash them. Then they were put in to soak, in to starch, and then she'd take them, and they'd nearly stand on their own on the window.

"There used to be lines in the yard. Rows of white sheets drying." [6]

And she used to do the same with the sheets, and at that time all sheets, they were all white, there was no coloured sheets then, and me mother used to do the sheets as well, and the starch, and in the winter, getting into the bed, I used to say to me mother, the sheet would be stiff, and they'd be icy cold, and I used to say to her, 'Ma, I wish you didn't starch the sheets' because they were icy cold coming down on top of me, you know. It was desperate! And the pillow cases were the same. You could buy the pillow cases with lovely fringe around them, at that time, up in Frawley's and all, and in O'Hora's of Francis Street. There used to be a shop called O'Hora's, and you could buy your bed clothes and all there, and when people would starch their bed clothes, because you'd see them all out on the line in the yard, they used to have big lines in the yard, and next thing they'd take them in, and they'd be drying, and then they were starched, they were stiff, the lace on the pillow cases, then the sheets, and then they'd have a white quilt on the bed, it used be gorgeous now, you know.

6. See page 229

'Monday Morning' by Hugh Doran - Hugh Doran Collection. Photo courtesy of the Irish Architectural Archive.

DUBLIN HOUSES COLLAPSE

THREE PERSONS KILLED

THREE persons were killed and fifteen others had to receive hospital treatment when two houses collapsed in Old Bride street, Dublin, shortly after 10 o'clock yesterday morning. A third house partly collapsed.

The dead are: Mrs. Bridget Lynskey (30) and her five-months-old baby, Noel, and Samuel O'Brien (72), a pensioner of Messrs. Guinness. They all lived in the tenement house, No. 46 Old Bride street.

Several of the families—there were five families in all—living in No. 46 were preparing to move to new homes in the immediate future. Mrs. Lynskey, the dead woman, had the key to a new Dublin Corporation house at Kimmage in her possession; she and her family were to have moved there to-morrow.

Patrick Hanvey, a 15-year-old member of the A.R.P. Emergency Communications Service, who lived in No. 47 Old Bride street—the second of the

26/158 Tenement House Collapses

It was just after 10 o'clock on the 1st June 1941 that No. 46 Bride Street collapsed.

It never, ever leaves you. you know, it's still with me, I can go over everything that happened that morning. We had gone to 8 o'clock Mass at Whitefriar Street, we went to Mass and the Holy Communion and you had to fast from the night before, and we were back and we had our breakfast. Then my mother had a pot on the gas, for the meat, that's what you did in those days you'd have something on. Mr. Lynskey had said there's something wrong here. And he came up to where we slept in the back room and just outside the window there was bricks falling off the wall down into the yard. They were kind of falling down and my mother said get out quick and we got down one flight and on the second flight I was getting down the stairs, I just put my hand on the banisters and they just came down. And because it was during the war as a child, an 8 year old I said when this stops now I'll be dead. I was covered in debris. Eventually Jim got me out. People from No. 45 came in and lifted me, someone else lifted me over the wall into the next house and carried me out to the ambulance. A woman came down with the jug of tea. I don't remember getting any but I can still see the jug. My mother was saying to Mr. Lynskey where's your wife and child. Unfortunately they had been in bed and they passed away. Mr. Samuel O'Brien he died in hospital. And the rest were taken around to the Adelaide or the Meath Hospital. I just got a cut on my leg.

The collapse took place on the same day as the North Strand bombings. It appeared on the front page of papers.

There was a lot of tenements around at that time and you know there was tenements in Digges Street and my mother had a friend living there and I used to be terrified if she was going, I used to be terrified going up the stairs because that was always in your mind, you know. After that I was more inclined to walk on the other side of the road than to pass a tenement building.

27/158 Moving From The Tenements

Sometime later after the tenement collapsed we got a Corporation flat, 1b Bride Street. Living in the flats was different to living in the tenements. In the tenements you were living in one room, even though people reared ten and

The Irish Times June 2 1941. Image courtesy of Mary Murtagh.

twelve children they all slept in the one bed. The tenement would have been about 100 years old. The plumbing – well you had two buckets, you had one for the slops and a white bucket for clean water. You had to go down to the yard; there were two toilets out in the yard and a cold tap that's where you got your water in the yard. And there was two toilets so you'd empty your slop into the toilet, flushed the toilet and then you had a tap in the yard you filled your white bucket with clean water and you washed your other bucket. But there was no toilets as your own toilet, you shared, the building was four-storied. There was the two sisters lived down on the bottom, Mrs. Lynskey then and my Uncle Joe, then we had that back room and the O'Briens had the front room and they had the whole top and they could have had water up there, I think they had a kind of a kitchen on the landing because they were up the top.

In the Corporation flats on Bride Street you had a toilet of your own and you had a cold tap. You had two bedrooms a small room people called a scullery, a kitchen and you had a front room.

War Stories – Sent Out

He went away to England in 1939. They were looking for soldiers then. He was in the air forces, he wanted to be a pilot, but he failed the eye test, you know, it had to be perfect sight then. John went through all the war and me mother, I don't know how she lived through it, because she was up in John's Lane I think every day of the week, lighting lamps to the Mother of Good Counsel, going to Mass every day. John went back to England anyway, and next thing he was sent out. He was in Germany and then he went to Singapore, he was in Burma, and then he was in a place called Rangoon, because I have an old letter here that he sent to me mother, and now it's falling to bits, but it was from Rangoon you know. John wouldn't even write away for his medal, and he had the Burma Star, he got the Burma Star and all, but he wouldn't write away for it, and my mother would say to him, 'Why don't you write?' 'No, I've enough memories,' he always said.

1940s

John Donnelly. Photo courtesy of Harriet Donnelly.

Army Newsletter sent home by John Donnelly. Image courtesy of Harriet Donnelly.

29/158 Table Manners

The way we were brought up, you didn't speak unless you were spoken to, you know, even at the table. We were often sitting at the table, and me brother, James Donnelly, he was a devil for that, he used to look at me and he'd be kicking me under the table, because you couldn't speak at the table, 'Stop that talking,' me father would say, 'Don't insult God's good food, eat and then talk,' he used to say. So we had to just eat our dinner, you couldn't talk, but gradually through the years, as we got older, we did. One night me father was reading the paper and we were all at the table. During the war, he used to read the paper to my mother because she couldn't read, and it was mostly about the war, especially when John was away in the army. So this particular night he was reading a story and he happened to say, '… and Lord Haw Haw' I was drinking tea and I spluttered and said, 'Haw Haw!' I thought it was hilarious, and me other brother started to laugh, and me father was disgusted. 'Stop that, at the table, be quiet,' and he started off again, and of course when it came to mentioning Lord Haw Haw we were, the two of us off again, in stitches. I'm telling you like we weren't allowed to talk at the table never mind laugh, as you were insulting what was on the table. See the parents years ago were so thankful to God that they had food on the table, you know, and if you knew anyone around like that hadn't anything, everyone shared with one another, you know.

.... 1940s

$\frac{30}{158}$ Rations

An ounce of butter. That was our ration. When you went to buy anything they would take your ration book off you. The Government supplied them to everybody. They took the name and address like you get your voting papers. They sent the ration book with your name and address on it. They'd send it out to you in the post, but you only got the one ration book, but you could use it for your stamps but you never got anymore until the following week. We only had the little sup of tea and a little bit of butter, a quarter of butter to last you for a week and baking the bread it was browny colour, never a bit of white bread. We were lucky compared to what some people had. Only for the merchant navy we wouldn't have got that. They went out through the fighting an' all to get the supply of food for us, they did. Only for the merchant navy we wouldn't have even got that.

A 1940s ration card. Image courtesy of Chris Reid.

31/158 The Telegram Boy

There was a family that lived at the top of the house, Mrs. Lyons, all her family, and her sons was the same as my brother, they had joined the British Army, and at that time, when anybody was killed, or wounded, the telegram boys used to come, and every time me mother saw a telegram boy, she'd nearly faint with the fright, in case they were coming to her, you know. On this particular day, she saw a telegram boy, he came up into the hall and she met him on the stairs, and she just froze, you know. But he passed her, and went upstairs. It was Mrs. Lyons' son. He'd been killed in the war, it was very sad, you know. Mrs. Lyons other son, Danny, had joined as well, but he came through it and lived in England after the war. Himself and John, my brother, whenever they'd be home on leave at the same time, they'd be talking to each other, because they both knew and understood each other.

"During the war whenever a local man was killed or wounded the telegram boys used to come. One day my mother saw the telegram boy. She met him on the stairs. She almost fainted. But he passed her and went to another woman on the next floor." [7]

32/158 Censored Letters

When the war was over, we hadn't heard from him for weeks, me mother was all upset, and then a letter arrived and we finally got word. The letters used to take so long to get here and often almost everything was scratched out. They weren't allowed to mention anything about the war and even the least thing was scratched out. Often you were trying to put all the words together, to try and figure out what the letter was about actually, because you'd read one line, and the next line would be, you know, a line across it, you couldn't see it, and as I said it took weeks, sometimes a couple of months, for it to get here. We knew that the war was over of course, everyone knew, and we said, 'He'll be getting demobbed now.' So then finally the letter came, that he was coming home.

7. See page 229

33/158 Another Letter

My mother used to go down to a nun in an enclosed order on Leeson Street. The nun used to say, 'No news is good news'. My mother got a letter first, that he was reported missing, and he was missing for about eighteen months, and then after she got official word, that they had found the body. He was shot, then I think they dragged the bodies in, into farmland and that, you know. When the war was over they took the bodies out, and when the bodies came, they gave them all their burial and they gave them all their own graves and that and me mother got an envelope one morning with all his stuff back in it, his belongings, photographs. I have a photograph up there of his grave in Belgium. I was going to school at the time; he was the eldest of the family. I was only about nine or ten when the Second World War broke out. And as matter of fact me brother – he went over to see me eldest brother's grave in Belgium. Danny went when he got his retirement out of the job; he went over to see the grave. Me brother. He was older than me, yea, and me brother that's younger than Danny, he's in Rugby, they're the only two brothers I have left, and meself. Well he was on the Home Guard, they had to keep the enemy out, or go in front. I don't like to go by when me brothers are talking about it.

34/158 He Had Enough Memories

No, never wrote away for his medal, he never wanted them, he said, 'No'. And I said to Olive, his wife, 'Did he never write'? 'No,' she said. 'Well he should have,' I said, 'because there's his son now, he could have had them.' 'No,' she said, 'he always said he has enough memories, he doesn't need medals to remind him and he tried to forget the memories, you know'. You tried to ask him about his memories, and you'd say like 'What did you do?' he just shook his head, you know. I mean we had his letters and all, and as I said, whatever it was he told us it was scratched out. You couldn't even pick up anything from the letters, but they're all from all the places he was in. I often wondered, it must have been horrendous. He couldn't even speak about it.

35/158 He Wouldn't Talk About It

After he was demobbed and all, he wouldn't talk about his experiences in the war, once when he came back from Japan, and we said, 'What about Japan?' he said, 'Oh, the children, the children,' and he wouldn't tell you about the children; they were starving you see, and they used to follow them and sometimes the soldiers used to give them their rations. 'They were hungry, they were starving,' he used to say, and there wasn't an ounce of flesh on them. This was in Japan at the end of the war, and they sort of had to go back in, troops for to organise everything, but like he could never talk about it. It had an awful effect on him.

Talk about it. Never. Me father used to ask him questions and he used to say to me mother, 'I can't get a word out of him' and me father was going mad to know – he was interested naturally because he was in the First World War, and me mother used say to him, 'Ah look, it wasn't like when you were in the army, in the last war.' 'Oh yes,' he used to say, 'Sure we didn't suffer at all,' he used to say to me mother, 'You think this war is the worst,' and she said, 'Yes, well there's planes and bombs and everything now.' But like me father, both himself and my brother did go through the mill.

36/158 Demobbed

During his time in England he had met a girl. When he'd be on leave here, he'd spend so much time here, and then he'd go back to England to spend the rest of his leave with her. So anyway instead of going straight to her, now fair play to him, when he was demobbed, he knew the state me mother was in, he came straight home here. The last place he was in was Japan, and he came straight home then, even though he also had to go back to England to sort out his papers and all.

37/158 Home Front

When he lived in England, I often went over to him for a holiday, and I used to notice when there'd be a war film on, he used to always go out of the room. After a while like I started to think it was because he was in the war, you

Bronze Plaque installed on Nicholas Street. Story nos. 9, 28, 34 & 35/158. See no. 3 on page 8 and 9. Photo by Chris Reid.

My father was in the British Army during the 1st World War. He got some medals but when he left the army he pawned them and never redeemed them. My brother, he was in the British Airforce during the 2nd World War. My father was mad to know about it. He used to say to my mother, 'I can't get a word out of him'. My brother got the Burma Star and all, but he never even wrote away for his medal. He said he didn't need medals to remind him.

know. I asked him one day he said 'Ah, yea, Hollywood – it wasn't like that. It wasn't glamorous like that,' that's all he would say. My sister noticed that too about John and she said it to Olive his wife, that a friend of John's in the Air Force was killed. She said he saw his friend getting blown to bits, and that's why he would never look at a war film, he always used go out, you know. He was a very gentle person, but when he lost his temper, oh, he was fierce, you know, every part of him would go, he was very emotional. He never even came to me mother's funeral, he wouldn't go to a funeral, because he gets too emotional, not able to control his emotions.

38/158 Minding Big Houses

I was in the Irish Army for five years during the war. The Irish Army was mobilised at that time. I was in what was called the volunteers and the reason I was in the volunteers was I never had a holiday in my life. I was 19 years of age at that time so by joining the volunteers I used to get a fortnight every year up in Gormanstown; that's why I joined. I was in my teens only in the volunteers. When I got called up I was only 19. 1939. I joined the volunteers then I was in the army at that time. Had a good big gang around me and all that carry on, you know, them fellas and a half dozen more of them. I got on very well. I was offered an extra stripe if I stopped in the army; I told them what to do with it. We were all over, we used to be accompanied up to the out-posts you know. We were in the Midlands, Longford, Athlone and that. Then our company was taken from the battalion. We used to do all of Sligo, Letterkenny; we'd go in there maybe for a month or two and then were moved on. Often we used to be in the mansions – beautiful, absolutely, you should be in some of those places, the spiral staircases and all this carry on. They were all vacant, we were in one in Sligo, I can't remember what one, I can't remember their names. I don't know now who lived there, who owned them, but I do know that we never stopped in a barracks. Always in one of those big houses, one was in Letterkenny, I was trying to think of the name of it I can't remember, there was another one in, was it, Boyle, Boyle Co. Roscommon. But as I say we were all heartbroken when we were pulled back into the barracks after living in the mansions.

Free State Army identity card. Image courtesy of Aileen Morrissey.

39/158 Uncle

Me mammy's mother was an Argentinian woman. My father was a Protestant man from England, Prior was his name. My father and his brothers were all in the war. The Second World War. This uncle, he had malaria fever and he was brought home. His mother looked after him during his malaria fever. They were living in rooms in the tenements in Messrs Street, up in the tip top floor. Seemingly back in them days they used to call potatoes 'poppies'. Anyway my uncle died from the malaria fever and he was laid out in their rooms in the tenements on Messrs Street. He lay in his coffin – dead. They had got him ready for the burial the next morning. Relations, friends and neighbours were all sitting around drinking and having a sing song when he sat up in the coffin and shouted, 'I want poppies! I want poppies!' Everyone jumped – pandemonium – all on top of one another, tumbling down the tenement stairs in the dark. People ran screaming in the street. A priest was brought, the whole lot. He lived, I believe, for a few years. His mother refused to look after him. She wouldn't say why. She got the person below in the flat below to look after him. He was well looked after but he died after a while. The Mother was happier about it then. But they made sure he was fecking dead then. They bet him down to see if he was dead. They didn't want the same thing to happen again.

1940s ....

40/158 A Good Social Life

I had a good social life, yea, before I settled down. I seen life first. This is it, don't settle yourself down too soon. Me sister married a chap from Green Street and it was through him that I met me husband. You see you were always meeting like, there was always birthday and wedding parties going, and you'd be invited and meet someone there. I think Rosaleen met Peter through a birthday party in the flats, and it was through Peter then she got to know my future husband and he used to come over to Bride Street, and then it was through them that I met him. I think he was to do best man for me sister, but then someone else asked him... You see there was always something going on, there was always dances going. I danced at Parnell Street, I danced in the Ierne for céili. Ballroom dancing, we always danced the ballroom at the Metropole, and the Crystal Ballroom off Grafton Street. I danced up in the Palace, I danced in the Olympic Ballroom in Pleasant Street. Every week we went, we went to the Olympic every Saturday night. I've often danced twice, say the afternoon, and then went again on Sunday night to a dance. I had a great social life. And then we were always at the pictures, and theatres. We used to go a lot to the Queen's Theatre. I used to go to the Royal every Friday with me pal. They used always show the picture after, and I went to the Gaiety to see plays there. We went to the Olympia. And they used to have a lovely talent on the Queen's, on a Sunday night. Plenty of pals, like when I worked in Kavanagh's there was always tickets going for dances. Somebody would come in with a ticket and you'd go to a dance, you meet someone there, you'd introduce this person to that person. There was no such thing as only going out the weekend, like you see them now, I do see them nowadays, and I think they work all the week to go to the pub on a Thursday night, Friday night, you won't see anyone around Saturday night or Sunday night, back to work again until Thursday, go off out again, buy drinks and that, and we never drank in them days, you know, but we enjoyed ourselves great. I think I was out every night of the week. I'd have been in me twenties.

Bronze Plaque installed on Nicholas Street. Story no. 40/158. See no. 6 on page 8 and 9. Photo by Chris Reid.

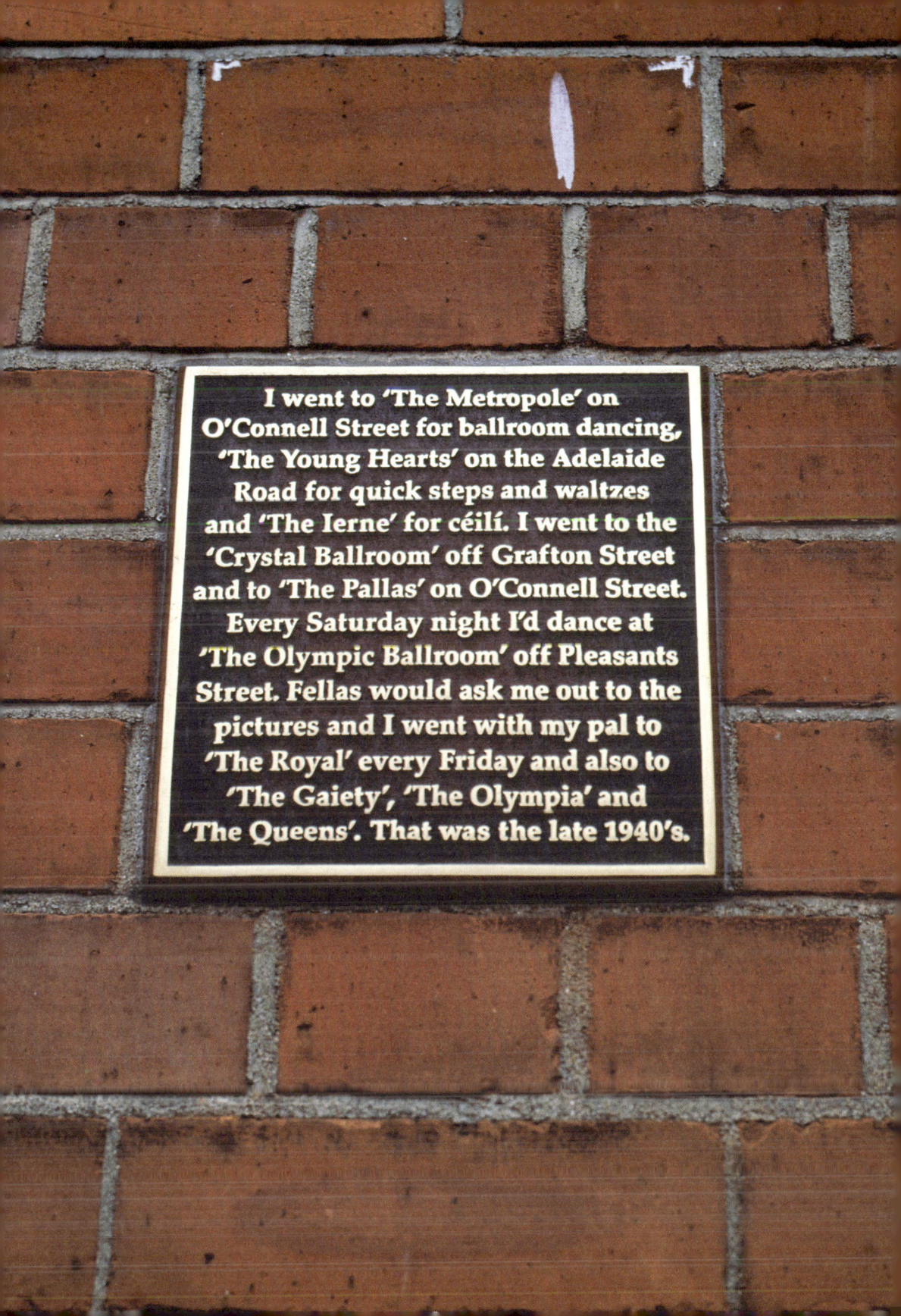

I went to 'The Metropole' on O'Connell Street for ballroom dancing, 'The Young Hearts' on the Adelaide Road for quick steps and waltzes and 'The Ierne' for céilí. I went to the 'Crystal Ballroom' off Grafton Street and to 'The Pallas' on O'Connell Street. Every Saturday night I'd dance at 'The Olympic Ballroom' off Pleasants Street. Fellas would ask me out to the pictures and I went with my pal to 'The Royal' every Friday and also to 'The Gaiety', 'The Olympia' and 'The Queens'. That was the late 1940's.

They had seven children and decided this was enough. One day after mass, she arrived home and told her husband that the priest said no one of childbearing age should stop having children. Sometime later she had another. Both she and the baby died during the birth. They were buried together.

41/158 Family Planning

He got married first and his wife had seven lovely children. She came home. That time there was Missions' retreat that lasted for a fortnight. A fortnight for the men and a fortnight for the women and the priest/missioners used come from a different country. They'd jump out of the pulpit and tell you'd roast in hell. The poor girl went to the Mission. She had seven children and he was the best husband in the world. They were going together since school. When they were 20 or 21 they got married and they had seven children, seven lovely children, good looking children. One year she went to the Missioners one time and they told her, 'Anyone of childbearing age has to bring children into the world.' The poor girl came home and thought she was living in sin. She came home and said to her husband, 'The Missioner is after giving out from the pulpit that anyone that is childbearing should have them and is not supposed to stop. That God sends them.' They had another child. He didn't want to. He said, 'We don't want anymore. We have enough children. We have seven, that's enough.' But she said, 'It's not right if you can have children, you can't put it off.' Anyway she had the baby. She was in the old Coombe hospital. They had a baby boy. The boy died, then she died and she and the baby was buried together.

You had to open your eyes. That woman wouldn't have had another child. I thought it was a terrible thing when I heard the story. I thought what right had they to tell her to have a child or not to have a child. They had no right them, giving out on the Mission and them carrying on themselves. Just going into the confession box and telling them your sins, the same fellows were doing worse themselves. I don't blame the young people for not liking the priests. I have no time for them.

42/158 I Was Very Innocent...

My mother had a baby in 1945. I remember the doctor came down the stairs. He told us he had brought a little baby sister to us and we were delighted.

Sometime later, I was just seventeen, I emigrated to England and got work. There was a staff hall where we used to have our meals. One day these English girls sat next to me. They were laughing and joking and we were having the craic. One said to me, 'Was your mother ever up the pole?' I turned to her and

Bronze Plaque installed on Nicholas Street. Story no. 41/158. See no. 1 on page 8 and 9.
Photo by Chris Reid.

said, 'My mother never climbs poles.' True, I thought, but the other girls were laughing and laughing and I got so embarrassed and sick I cried to myself all day long.

When the Matron asked what was wrong I told her and she challenged the girls. 'Why don't you leave her to her innocence?' she said, 'she doesn't know what you meant by that.' When they told me what it meant I couldn't believe them. The Matron explained that it meant that the doctor did not bring the babies. 'But,' I said, confused, 'I came out of a head of cabbage.'

The Matron couldn't believe it. I had been working a long time there when one day she told me, 'I really couldn't understand,' she said, 'you were very, very innocent.' Everyone was the same, or so it seemed. Me sisters and all, were the same. I suppose it was the way we were brought up. We weren't told anything about life. We were brought up to be thick to be honest with you.

Irish in England

Because the girl John married was a Protestant they couldn't be married on the high altar. So we had to go up to Drimnagh where my aunt lived, and go to the church up there, the Mother of Good Counsel church. They were married in the vestry, not out on the altar because that's the way it was then but he was satisfied, they were married in the Catholic Church.

He worked as a welder and reared his family in Yorkshire, England. He had two children, Janet and Stephen. The kids are married with families of their own now, but like the place where he was working, he worked there for years, and he had great hands. John could do anything, he even made his own television set, because they couldn't afford to buy a new one, and he bought all the parts and put them all together. It was beautiful, and a beautiful cabinet he built around it.

I used to go visit him. On Sunday morning he would bring us up to the church, St. Pat's. It was a bit away from the house, but it wasn't too far, so we walked to it. And that was before his son and his daughter all got cars. And we used to walk up to it and then when we would get to it the first thing that struck me, the first time I went to it. All the men standing outside the church and their caps, and I said to John, they look like Irish men and he said they are. They are all Irish. From the country and everything and they all made

Five children who lived in Bride Street in the 1940s. Back (left to right): David McFadden, Fergus Redmond, Seán Redmond. Front (left to right): Marie Redmond, Irene Redmond. Photo courtesy of Fergus Redmond.

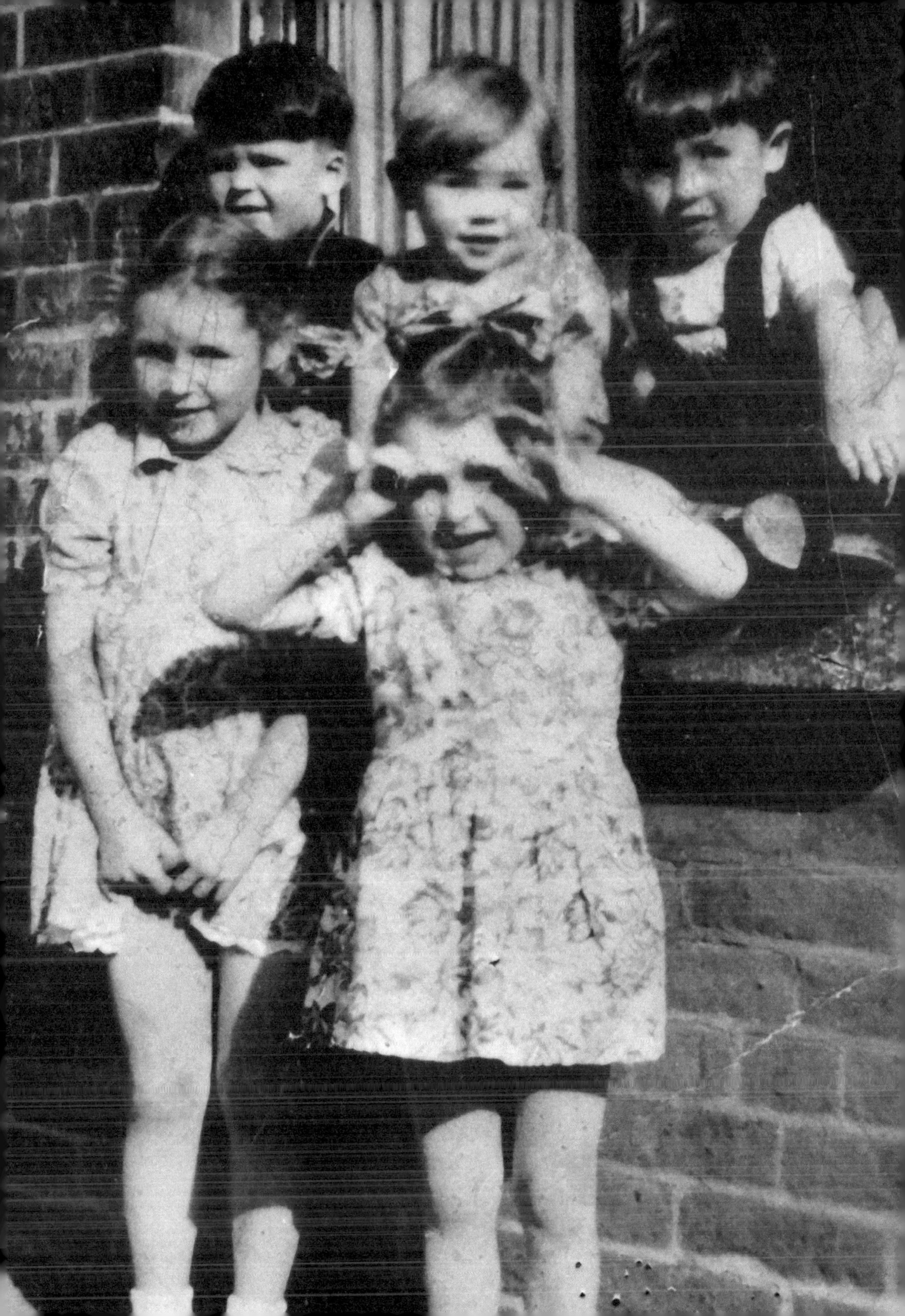

their way up the same path to St. Patrick's on Sunday morning. And they would all be outside chatting and having their smoke and everything. And the same after the Mass they would be chatting then and they would all go off to the pub or something. And it was amazing that there was that many Irish people in Yorkshire, you know.

The Bayno — England in Ireland

We used to all go there. Elisa Lynch – She was the head that woman. We used to be groomed in the corner and she'd be playing piano. And they had the may pole out in the yard and there was all different colours, ribbons. We were all only small. And we would all grab one of the ribbons, now there was hundreds of them on the may pole. But it was a huge big pole. And you would be going around and you would be singing songs, going in and out and keeping time. 'Weave' – The teacher would be telling us what to do, you know. They used to teach us dancing and marching up and down this big room and singing songs. And it was owned by the Guinness family, you know. And the Queen and all was here, or was it the king. Came over, that was when we were all under the English rule you know. Funnily enough I would like to see the Queen coming. Not because I am mad British just do you know what I think about Ireland and England, they are like two separate branches of a family. Two different branches and there is a love/hate relationship. And it's like they are my family and they are my cousins and they would give you a pain. You know that way. The present royal family are not like they were years ago, they have had to change you know. Years ago they did treat Ireland in a terrible way. You know, the time of the famine especially, you know, it was terrible. And it all stems from that, all this hatred; they had Ireland under the thumb. There is as much Irish in England as there is in Ireland. Liverpool was called Dublin's overflow.

Children arriving with their parents at the Bayno, 1954. Photo courtesy of the Guinness Archive, Diageo Ireland.

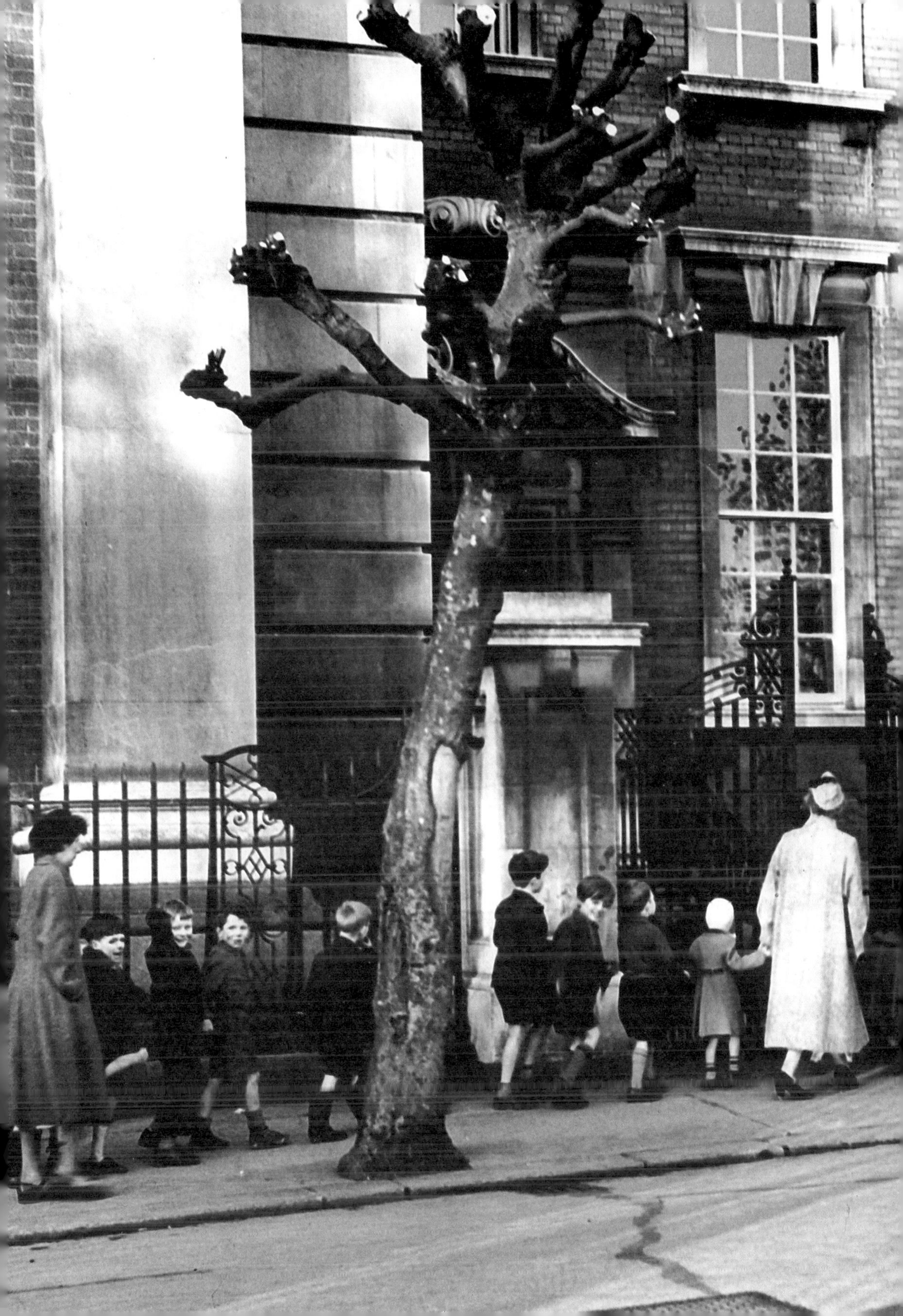

19

Children playing in the yards off the Ross Road, 1950s. Photo by Neville Johnson. ©RTÉ Stills Library.

50s

1950s

One of Thirteen

I'm one of thirteen children in a family that was reared on the Ross Road. I'd ten brothers and two sisters and meself and me Ma and me Da. And as the years went on, me Ma lost three of the brothers and then there was ten of us in a two bedroomed flat, me granny's flat. And me granny had her own place, her own room, and we were all squashed in the other room. Me Da made bunks, three sets of bunks up to the ceiling; the baby would be in a cot he'd be after making. I was in one of the top ones. Then there was great neighbours – Moggy Dalton. When my mum went in to have her babies, Moggy would take the washing, Mrs. McCabe would take the girls and Mrs. Power would take the boys. They were me neighbours, there was roughly about, well there was ten of us (the Slymans), there was about seven of the Powers, there was thirteen of the Gibbons, I think there was about six Hoeys, six Eustaces and three McCabes in one Hall, and then there was Moggy's across the road. There was Maggie Byrne, she had about ten children, Mrs. Connaughton, she had about eight, Mrs. Forte had four, Mrs. Glennon had four, Moggy had six or seven, Mrs. Hand had about six. They were the end houses on the Ross Road, near at the Bride Street, Number 11 and Number 1. Facing each other and if anything was going on, on the road or anybody, if anything ever happened on the road, everybody in them two halls looked out for all the kids' right.

Games and Schools

They'd play all types of games. Relievio. They played Beds – like you'd have round polish tins and your lines and on one foot you'd push the round tin into another open and you'd keep going around. They played Beds. They played marbles. They played games like you know where the water stopcock is, they'd open that and play a thing called hoe. You'd try and get your coins in. There were all sorts of games like that. But Relievio was a great game because it gave you an opportunity of running through the open doors and halls. Sometimes a resident wouldn't like it – a crowd of children chasing in. But it was great. Some of the children went to Francis Street School. Some of them went to St. Michael's and John's. Some of them went to St. Audoen's, which would've been originally right on the city walls. The great thing about it was you were near everywhere. I went to school in Francis Street because it was the nearest. Usually you went to the school in your parish.

"We'd draw squares with chalk on the ground, with numbers in them – 1, 2, 3, 4, 5, 6. We'd use a round, flattish empty tin. You'd throw it – if it landed on square 4 you hopped up into 4. Then you kicked it into the next number up – square 5. Then you hopped into 5 and tried to kick it into the next one. Depending on how many you were able to get you won." [8]

Names and Unlocked Doors

In most cases if you weren't known, they'd look at you, because many of the doors wouldn't be locked. There was always someone there – the granny perhaps – but so many of the doors were unlocked. The children wouldn't have had a key to the door or anything. At certain times the parents, usually the mother, would call them in. As families were large, often a list of names would be called. They'd shout out the names – Johnny, Paddy, Tommy, Mary – and the children might say, 'Right I'll have to go or I'll get a hiding.' It would've been done several times a day. It would have been done for tea time and for going to bed.

I Grew Up on The Ross Road

I was born in 1954. I don't remember me childhood as being overly happy. Growing up it was tough enough; it wasn't easy you know – no money. Things were tight, six or eight in the family, my mother died when I was twelve and there was two younger than me. Me father, he was a labourer. He drank a lot, so that made it harder, yea, so as I say it was hard times. But they did work, there were very few men who didn't work, you know working class meant working class, they did work, they worked and they drank.

8. See page 229

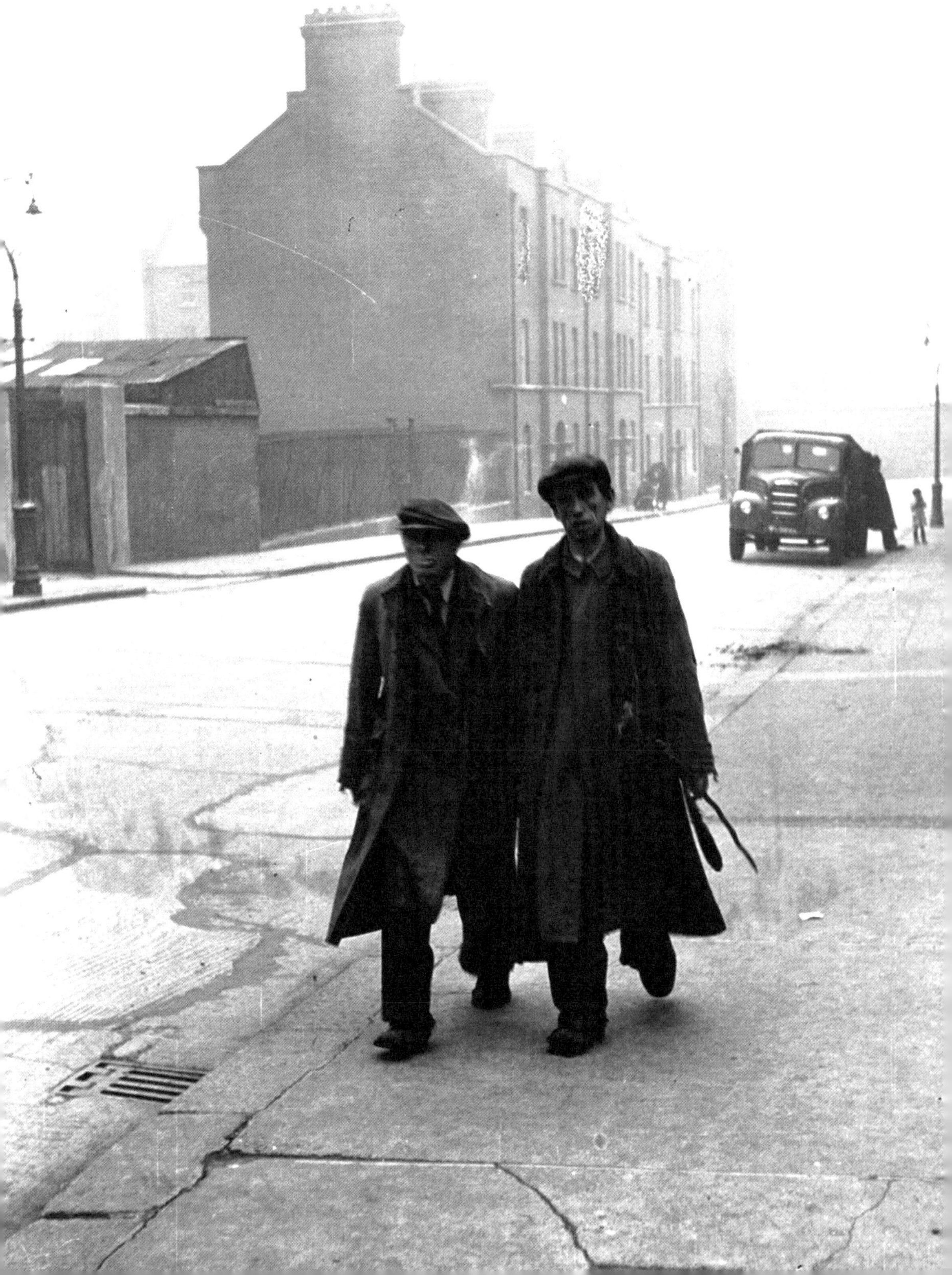

We lived in a two bedroomed flat. I suppose it was cramped but that's what you grew up with you see. Bunk beds and two or three to a bed. You were washed in a tin bath on Saturday night by your mother, and it was very eco-friendly, because we all shared the one water. Yea, the big auld tin bath, and you got your clothes changed. I learnt to swim in the Iveagh Baths. I remember I was so small when I started going to the Iveagh Baths, there was a little hatch that you paid the money in, like a little round window, and I was small enough that I didn't reach up to the window, and I had to reach up me hand to give in me shilling, or whatever it cost, I was that small. And that was on the left hand side as you go in the doors there.

There was no cars on the Ross Road, nobody had a car, now you couldn't park on the road, you couldn't get in – It's full of cars! Nobody had the phone. I don't think there was a phone on the whole of the Ross Road. Went into the pub, and used the phone there, if you had to make a phone call.

Games

There was roughly about, there was the best part of nearly fifty kids in our hall, there was about a hundred kids between two halls (1 Ross Road and 11 Ross Road), all that Ross Road I'd say there must have been about, Jaysus, the best part of 200 to 250 kids on that road playing. Always playing marbles, piggy, your Da would be looking for the shoe polish, it was gone, spin the bottle. Beds, hop, hop, hop, you know, and skipping. We were always playing and the kids were happier; we never had any swinging boats or anything, where you got the swinging boats were in the Bayno. Yeah all the swings and things and the whole lot, the sandpit and the whole lot.

Then there'd be times me and me friend would be going down to the docks to help the culchies up onto the boat to get a few shillings to bring home to our Ma and I'd have two babies in a pram and she'd have one baby, and at the end of the night after the ship going off we'd be sitting on the steps of the Liffey and I'd be washing the babies feet in the Liffey. This was my two little brothers. Washing their feet but then when the shampoo came out it came out in a sachet, right, and my friend she had ringworm in her hair so she had lost all her hair but her sister had lovely thick hair but we didn't know what happened, right. But her sister was in the doll's pram, she was so tiny she was in a doll's pram but she had loads of hair and we bought a sachet of the shampoo, instead of giving the money to our Ma we kept the money for the sachet of shampoo it was nine pence, right. And we brought her down to the Liffey and we got a hold of her, I held her legs while she was washing her hair in the Liffey water.

John Freer and his sister Margaret Freer enjoying the Phoenix Park in the 1950s. Photo courtesy of the Freer family.

⁵⁰⁄₁₅₈ Two Pools

Tara Street had two swimming pools, one for boys and one for girls, so you had a better chance of getting into Tara Street swimming pool, sometimes you'd get to Tara Street and you would have just missed the hour, say three o'clock, and you'd have to wait 'til four o'clock to get in and at this stage you'd be fed up and when four o'clock came you wouldn't get in so we used to end up down at the bridge fed up and at this stage I'm not sure how old I was, could have been ten or eleven but we would have started to ramble from that bridge to the docks. The docks to us at that time was Guinness boats, small boats would have boxes and barrels, there was no freight. As kids we rambled down and then we would be dancing on barrels or something, but as kids we weren't aware of the danger of what we were actually doing and we were always leaning over the arches to look at the water to see if there was anything in the water. By the time we rambled down we had probably been in trouble several times but we didn't mind, we just kept walking.

Rambling

I remember it was a hot summer's day we took our shoes and socks off and we were sitting by the horse trough having a great time and really enjoying ourselves, unaware of what we were doing except that our feet were tired and our feet were sore after a long walk and it was a hot summer day, and sitting dangling our feet in the water that the poor horses had to drink and a policeman caught us. We were terrified, he caught us by the scruff of our neck and I always remember my friend who was terrified and I would be a bit more brazen than her and when he asked us our name and address I remember giving him the name of a girl that was in my class and her address.

Finally when we got home you would be asked did you get a swim and of course you said yes but really you knew that you had actually been bold, you'd be terrified that you would be caught out and for weeks after the incident every time I seen a policeman I ran. I would have thought he was coming to tell my mother that I had been washing my feet in the horse trough. I think the poor woman would have died if she had known half things that we actually got up to.

The Sanatorium

I had been in hospital for two and a half years with rheumatic fever. Rheumatic fever is pains and aches all over your body and it left a strain on the heart. Probably from colds and different things like damp. They had a little sanatorium. It was like a convalescing home. This was when I was in hospital (Linden Convalescent Home, Stillorgan, Co. Dublin). I was told I was going for a new bike, because I was always robbing the bikes at the baths and I was told I was going for a new bike and when I was taken out to go to the sanatorium, we got a bus out to Stillorgan. When we left the bus, I said, 'Is it up this avenue ma, up this big long lane for a new bike? Sure you'd get it in the university shop in George's Street.' 'No, this is where you get it,' and when she got me in, the nuns just took me and dragged me up the stairs and 'There's your bed – get into that.' And I was screaming for me Ma and Da and the whole lot.

1950s

I wrote to her, 'Dear ma, when are you coming to collect me? If you don't come I'm going to run out.' I called it a prison. Because you used to be killed in it too, the nuns used to kill you, the nurses used to kill you. It was very strict, you only seen your Ma and Da once a week and as a child to be taken away from all your little brothers and sisters was a nightmare. Although you were sick but like you couldn't grasp it. Isolation – that was it.

53/158 The Tenements on High Street

That area from Patrick Street around to High Street and down to Thomas Street like and also especially between High Street, and where you come to top of Thomas Street was completely different. I was born by St. Audoen's Park there and recently I found a picture of the tenements where I was born, in a book. And my father is coming out the door. And you just wouldn't recognise it and it's completely different. There is an island there in the middle of the road now and it starts from the junction of Nicholas Street and goes down to the High Street, and that was actually full width of the street when I was a kid. And we used to go across to Tailors' Hall and Back Lane there, that brings you onto Nicholas Street. The tenements I was born in, they would have went about 1963 or 1964.

Everyone in the tenements used the same toilet and the toilet was down the backyard. And some people didn't bother and they threw it out the back window. Hygiene in the tenements was appalling and we only had an open sewer at the back of those tenements in High Street. There was a big cesspit. It was rotten and the smell was terrible, you know. And as a kid I didn't know they were open sewers. It was the same all around the Liberties and you would see the old people bringing the buckets down all around there. They had toilets then in the 80s.

Mother Redcaps was there in the back lane, yeah, and along there was Winstanley's where they made shoes. And there was a big sewing factory alongside that and there was a big fire years ago. There are photographs and I think people were killed in it actually. The building adjoining to Winstanley was some type of a clothing factory. Back Lane, that is where Tailors' Hall is, and that bring you onto Nicholas Street there. My father, Lord rest him, and his friend was a manager in Winstanley's.

Bronze plaque installed on Nicholas Street. See no. 7 on page 8 and 9. Photo by Chris Reid.

The hill was steeper, the street narrower. The surface was all cobblestones. When winter weather made them freeze, horses struggled to climb. Sparks flew from their hooves.

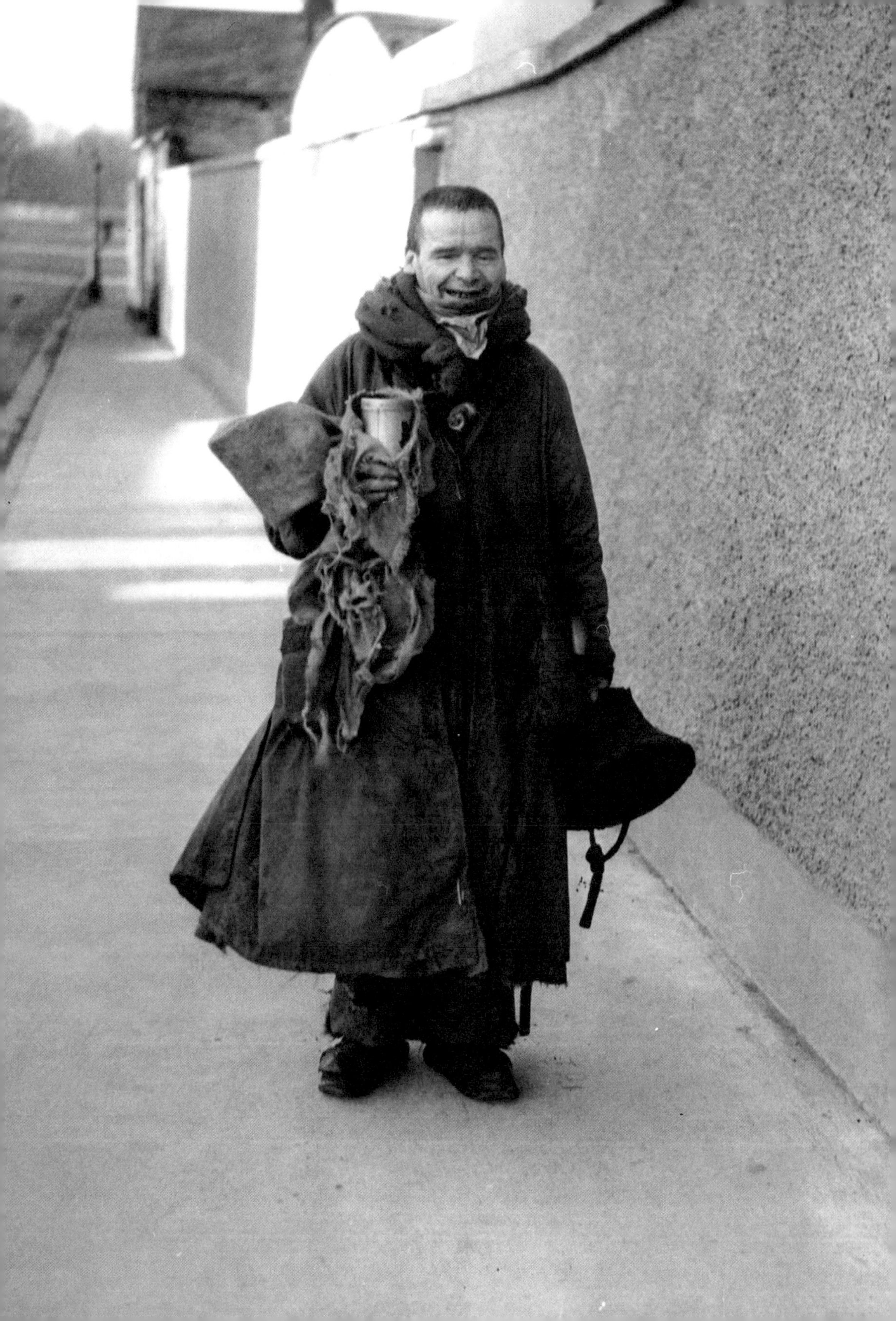

Christmas Dinner

It was Christmas and this one man was staying in the lodge – the Iveagh Lodge. He'd talk one time and then he wouldn't talk to you again. I remember I said to him, 'Christmas Day you can come to my house for your dinner.' I was about fourteen. He said no. 'Well,' I said, 'stand at the corner and I'll bring you down your dinner' and I used to see him all the time and it was Christmas Day and I went down the road, couldn't find him, walked up to the corner, couldn't find him, and he never came and I never saw that man from that day to this but sometime before he told me the story about the man and the newspapers. This other man lived in the hostel too, like some of them were live-ins and he used to be begging and all like that and he had so many newspapers stacked in the room and he died sudden and there was about 40,000 pound in that; it was right all along the walls and the ceilings, he had hidden the money there in the newspapers. That was an awful lot of money in those days and he was going around with no shoes like.

I'm not sure what they did with the money, but it wasn't unusual to see unusual people. It was the norm, you know, and everyone just went along as if that was it. It's not as if someone would stand out, because they were just part and parcel of the area.

Flower

He was a 'Jewman', a poor Jewman. This fella would always have a flower in his buttonhole and every day he would be rambling around. He was called Flower. He lived in the Iveagh Hostel. He always had a bag of currants; he used to give you currants if you were a kid. I used to get currants off him. And his flower – a nice flower. A flower in his button walking along. A small blocky man. He never minded anybody. Real quiet man. He would be well dressed, always well dressed. Never interfered with anyone, never spoke to anybody. Just walked, every time you'd see him he'd be walking around. He was a man withdrawn into himself. What happened to him or why he was like that I don't know. I was only a kid at the time. Never heard anything about the man. He just disappeared; of course being kids we didn't miss him.

> "He carried a stick because of his wooden leg. He would shout, banging the railings and ground with his stick. You would hear the clanging. He would wave his stick around or raise it in mid-air. Then he started to swipe at people. That was how it effected him – the war" [9]

In His Latter Years

He was one of the lodgers, poor unfortunate man. Mr. Lynch was his name and he had a wooden leg. I only vaguely remember him, as a kid, because he was very quiet after the war, but in his latter years then he got very aggressive. He had a stick, because he had a wooden leg, and I don't know anything about shell-shock but when I think about it now, was there any cure for it in them days. I don't think he ever got medical attention for that. He'd stand at the railings, and he'd bang his stick, and people were afraid of him in the latter years because he'd swing his stick, and he could hit you with it, no problem. Well he'd stand there, and he'd be shaking, the poor man, you know, and then bang the railings, or he'd bang the ground, and then he started hitting out. I seen him threatening, like I don't think he actually did hit anyone – people side-tracked him. His clothes were what you called Union[1], you always knew when these people came out of the Union, 'He's after coming out of the Union, because he has his Union suit on him.' Because it was like a uniform. Sometimes he'd be clean shaven, and other times he'd be beardy, he was never dirty because the baths[2] were there to get yourself washed..... He'd shout, 'Oh away with you, effin' bastards, and effin' Nazis' and things like that, you know. It could be to anybody, you know, and then you wouldn't be able to distinguish anything he'd be saying, because everything would be slurred because he'd be speaking so fast nothing made sense, because he was shell-shocked, very, very bad in the latter years. He had a walking stick, and he'd bang the railings. It was just his frustration, whatever shell-shock does to a man, that's what it was doing to this, that poor man. He had no family, none that I knew off. He wore shoes, though he had a wooden leg. I can't remember which leg was missing and I should remember, because his wooden leg ended

9. See page 231. *The Iveagh Baths on Bride Road.

up on the road, when he died. It was put in the bin, and the corporation must have dropped it out of the back of the van, and it ended up on the road, so I should really know whether it was the left leg or the right leg, can't remember. I think it was the left leg. It would be a brown shoe. I just remember seeing the leg, and one of the kids picking it up and running down Ship Street with it, and that's the last I saw of the leg.

57/158 Girls' School

I went to school at the convent. The nuns were very strict. I hated it, like my father took me out of it because he hated the nuns. They were very, very cruel, and they didn't know they were being cruel to me, now not like sexually or mentally, it was sort of physical cruelty, like smacking, and straps, and everything, especially the music teacher. You looked at the keyboard, you found your notes, and then you went on to reading the music. By a certain time you had to know how to read the music without looking at the keyboard. If I looked down, I got the whack of the belt so I stopped going to classes unbeknownst to my parents! I didn't go on the mitch, I just didn't attend music classes. When the bill was being paid, my father noticed that there was no music lessons fee on it, and wanted to know why. The nun sent for him, and told him that I wasn't interested in learning and he was just wasting his money, so I was taken out of it, and put into Marlborough Street School for my last two years. They realised my father was just wasting his money trying to educate me, I wasn't interested, I just hated the nuns, just didn't want to know, just wanted out of there. My father wasn't disappointed, because like the story I've heard now since, was my sister, that lives in America, she knew the way I was being treated down there, my sister told my father and mother that I was being abused down there, and that's the reason they took me out but I didn't care, I'm sorry now, I'm sorry now like I didn't continue with my education, I had the choice and I decided to work in my father's business.

"Of a Tuesday the women would be up washing their clothes in the wash house up beside the Iveagh Market. You carried your washing up and washed it in the basins, put

[1] A facility at Saint James's Hospital for homeless people
[2] The Iveagh Baths on Bride Road

1950s

it into a boiler, put it in the rinser and then brought it up the wringer. The clothes were then put on the big steel horse to dry them" [10]

$\frac{58}{158}$ Saturday at The Iveagh Market

The Iveagh Market was somewhere that your mother brought you on a Saturday and it was like her day out. Saturday you went. The dealers at the time, everything was lifted up item by item and people would bid on it and if you were lucky you came home with a new dress on a Saturday that your mother had bought for you in the Iveagh Market. As well we would go in and

10. See page 231

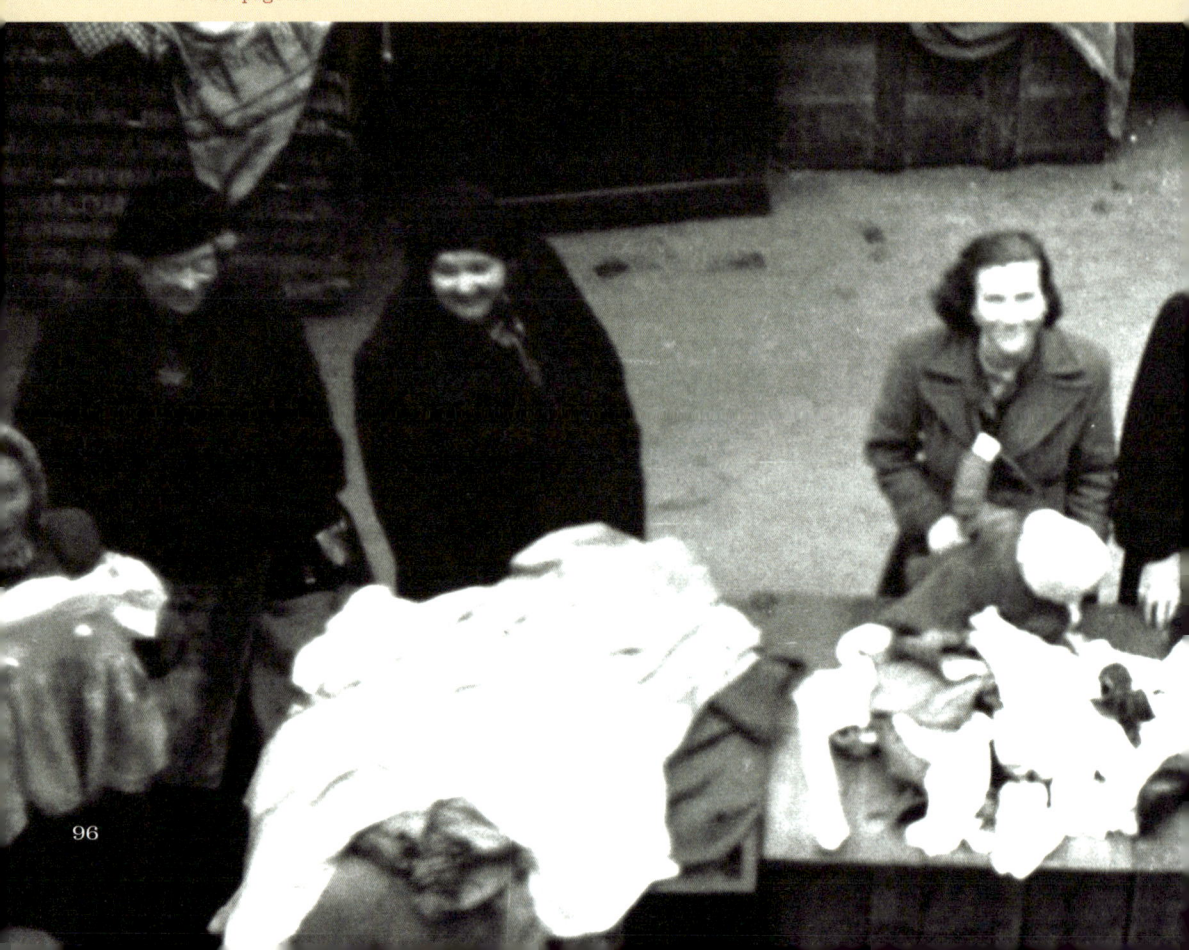

.... 1950s

play as kids and play hide and go seek until we were caught by the scruff of the neck, but it was always a place of mystery and we were always in trouble, the food market and the fish market down beside it. But the people in the Iveagh Market would be Mrs. Ward, if she caught you there she'd always send you for snuff.

I used to be up if me mother sent me up for messages there, that's the only time we'd go up and be running around it mad like just having a laugh. We'd be running up the stairs because it was so fascinating and you'd go up on the balcony and the clothes were there and then there was another balcony up further and you could look down and see all the things and the caretaker would be screaming, 'Don't fall off that balcony' and then he'd go to run and we'd run but I mean it was fascinating really when I think of it.

The Iveagh Market, 1954. Photo by Neville Johnson. ©RTÉ Stills Library.

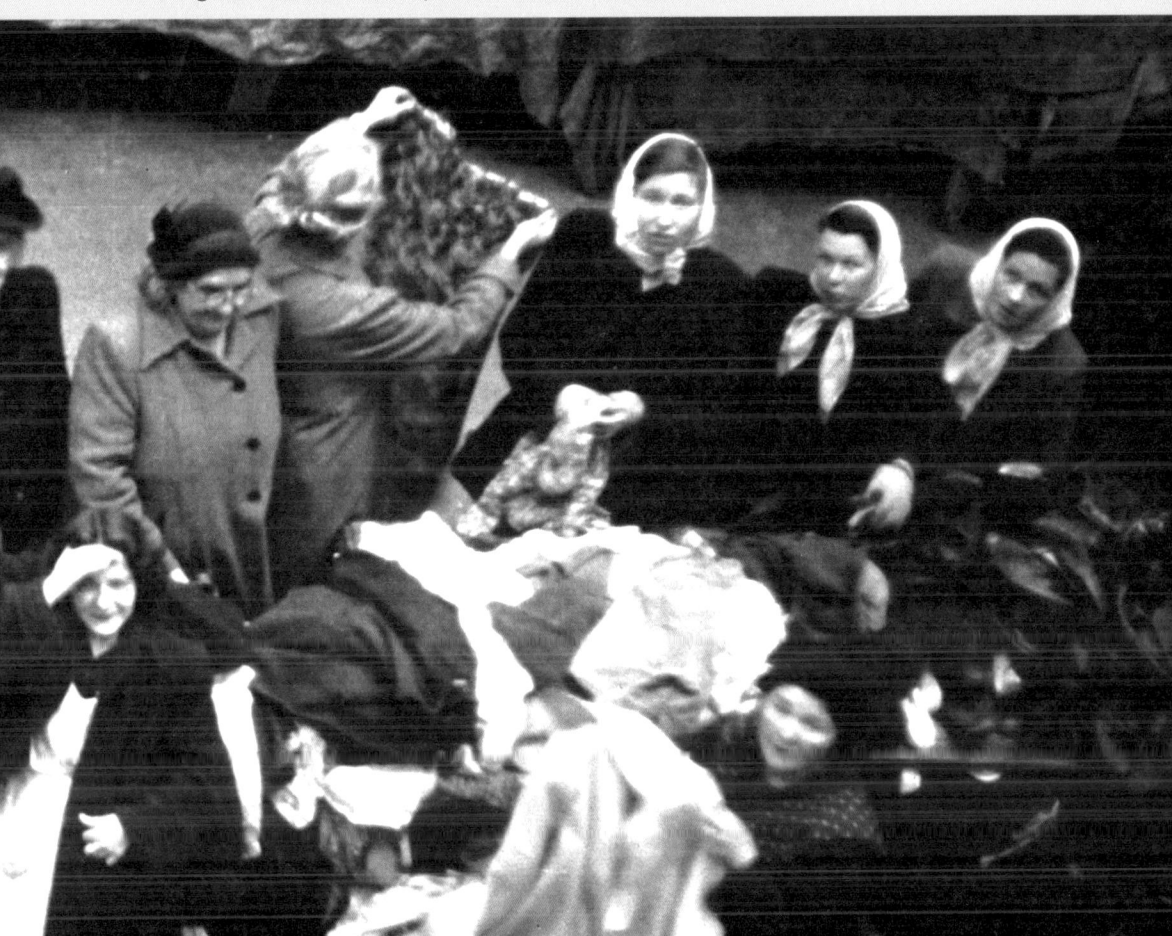

59/158 The Area — An Adventure Playground

As kids we used to play games on the street in the 1950s. Relievio, Kick the Can. We played out and went around the area – there was the Bayno, there was Stephen's Green, Patrick's Park. I mean when you're a young fellow, you know, sure you'd go anywhere, up to the canal to swim. Very little traffic, you could have your little, whatever you call it, the boxcars, and we used go down underneath the arch of Christchurch down to the river in the boxcars. There'd be loads of trips over to the Adelaide Hospital when you fell, and cut yourself, and hurt yourself, because you were always climbing. There was, where Jurys Hotel is now in Christchurch, they were all auld buildings and tenements, and you'd be climbing up them, and falling, falling through stairs, and looking for stuff. There's lots of tunnels underneath Christchurch, going back to the Penal Law times, and we'd go down into the tunnels. We often went, thirty or forty or fifty yards into them, it frightened the shite out of yourself though, but if we had an auld torch or candles, we found a skull one day, and played football with it in the yard, you know! And the children in the pram used to be left outside the window, and there'd be a bit of string tied through the window into the house, so the pram wouldn't move!

60/158 The Bayno

The Bayno was something that was there long before playschools or anything. It was owned by the Guinness family and it was way ahead of its years. We went to the Bayno every day after school and there was an outdoor playground. If you had a young sister you could leave her into the baby school for them to play. If you wanted to skip every child had a skipping rope. You could play ball, there was drama classes, dance classes, there was singing, there was cookery, there was a library, there was a big huge hall and you were all brought in every day and all of this every day, every child got a bun and a cup of cocoa in the big hall, big enamel jugs of cocoa. You got a bun and cocoa. You'd eat it as fast as you can and when the woman wasn't looking you'd change your coat or jumper, run back down to the seat, to ask for another. Come to the Bayno you'll get your burnt cocoa!

Children attending a class at the Bayno. Photo courtesy of the Guinness Archive, Diageo Ireland.

Every Christmas we had a massive Christmas party. You mightn't go to the Bayno for months but in the weeks up to Christmas you'd go so you'd get a ticket for the party, it was run by the Guinness family. There was a picture show at Christmas. We used to all dive in, it was a cowboy picture and all. You couldn't just show up, you had to get your ticket; you had to go a certain amount of times during the year. You had to go all the year round and then you'd get a ticket coming up to Christmas and the party, we used to get a bag of lemons – sweets, going in and you'd get a toy coming out after the film show off Santy. The toy was great; I got the wooden soldier.

61/158 Wild Children

There was some you wouldn't be allowed play with – I don't know why? There was more children then and some of them were wild and so you weren't allowed play with them like there's always a reason, just wild and went over the top. Then you know when you hear the name you say 'Oh God,' the name of the person, their surname and that. At the end of the day really they were just normal people. There wouldn't have been badness. It wasn't malicious or there was none of this real aggression that's now and the violence d'ye know what I mean, just normal wild.

They used to be robbing the gas meters and climbing up the spouts, gullies, scutting on the back of the lorries, you know the coal lorries, they'd rob a bag of coal and try and sell it, but you know people bought from them so they were as bad as the children when you think of it. And then there was a family who lived in the Iveagh Trust as well, sure they were notorious and one of them was extremely wild and it was very sad because one was sent to Daingean at that time and he escaped and I always remember his head was shaved and we were all playing in the square and didn't he come. We went crazy, He had escaped! We thought it was absolutely brilliant and he's back and then God love him the police came and took him away again. All his head was shaved. They had shaved his head and he looked real wild looking and then his mother and everybody was around and everyone was saying, 'You better not leave your key in the latch he's back,' but I mean his family was a very large family and most of those absolutely turned out fantastic.

I mean like you would have been put down years ago because you were poor and told you were stupid which you weren't. We just hadn't got the facilities, you know what I mean?

62/158 Everybody Just Mingled

My grandfather was British Army, my uncle was in the British Army. There was quite a lot around, retired like, and after the wars. We had a man lived beside us and he was British and he was after being a Colonel in the army. He lived in the Iveagh Trust and the reason he got the Iveagh Trust was he wanted to come to retire in Ireland and he got a flat there. And then you had Julia Coyne, her father was British Army and she was one of the brilliant swimmers.

.... 1950s

There was a lot that were British Army so like everybody just mingled, it was like the Protestants going to the Cathedral and going to the school, you'd be talking to them and up on Clanbrassil there were the Jews. Everybody was the same. There was no such thing as prejudice; it was lovely.

"It was sometime in the 1950s. We were all pals, we all worked together at 'The Two Owls' ladies and gentlemen's tailoring on Saint Augustine's Street. The girls got an idea one day at work to have a mock wedding. So we all dressed up and had a wedding." Photo and caption courtesy of Margaret Taylor.

Snobbery and Poverty

I just sort of found, what you call it, the snobbery was unreal. We weren't allowed to play with anybody really in Nicholas Street, only very few. I think a lot of the people thought that they were that bit better because they lived in the Iveagh Trust instead of Corporation but that is Ireland in my view. I find Ireland very snobby. I found people in the Iveagh Trust snobby.

There was some lovely people that lived on Nicholas Street but there were some mad people – they'd be more wild, the families would be more wild. There'd be big families, a lot of poverty, there was a lot of poverty in them because I even remember being in Whitefriar Street School and the teacher coming in one morning and asking them who had a breakfast before they came to school and the amount of children that had nothing was unbelievable so they kind of tried to look after them, so that was my first school. I went there when I was very young and I went to Clarendon Street. There was even a difference in the children in Clarendon Street. D'ye know, I don't know what it was but there seemed to be a lot of poverty. Now we weren't well off, but probably because me father had a steady job.

Buckets of Slop and The Cinema

Every penny counted. If children wanted to go to the Tivoli cinema you'd need four pence. To get this you'd collect buckets of slop – that was recycling before its time. You'd go to the nearest pig yard. There used to be one on Francis Street. It was four pence into the Tivoli and this woman would give us four pence for your bucket of waste. We'd go to each house or flat after dinner. What was left after dinner – potato peels, stale bread – cabbage wasn't as welcome. If you were clever and you hadn't filled a bucket you'd put the cabbage leaves on the bottom and slop at the top to rate it up. This was to feed the pigs. The woman on Francis Street was a bit blind and sometimes you'd catch her out. She'd think she was getting a full bucket with the slop at the top and cabbage leaves at the bottom. This way you could get two buckets out of one bucket of waste. You'd get eight pence instead of four pence and you'd go to the cinema. At the front they had wooden seats – wooheners. There was no barriers on them. You all sat together. There were all sorts of activities going on in the seats. Wasn't the most pleasant of places to be in. Some would get so excited by the film that they'd go to the toilet on the ground. They would be looking at it and wouldn't want to miss anything. They wouldn't have time to go to the toilet. You would have had Flash Gordon's trip to Mars, Hopalong Cassidy, Tom Nix, Roy Rogers, all of those and the children hated to see the nice little kissing. Children weren't interested. That'd always get a raspberry from the audience. Children weren't interested in that. They wanted drama, action, shooting.

65/158 Gas Man

When the gas man would come along I'd used to love that when they come to collect the meters then everybody they used to save in the gas meter and you might get three shillings back. I used to love that and then we'd all go to Killiney and we'd always have swiss roll. You could put an extra shilling in and if it was over the amount that was on the meter he'd give it back to you so when they had money they'd put it in, they knew that when he came that we would have a day out you know.

66/158 The Rag Man & Rag Woman

The rag man came around and used to come on his horse. He could have been anywhere. There was Woolfsons. I used to sell the jars too for the pictures and but there was different fellas that would come around. They might have a goldfish in a bowl or something and you'd be going pulling the place apart asking your mother for clothes. Many a good coat went, things that shouldn't have went, you'd give anything to the rag man and rag woman.

The rag woman she always came on a Friday. She had a big pram, a big baby's pram with a board on it, what you call those prams, they were like the boat shape. She'd have all the stuff on that like she'd have cups and saucers and little milk jugs and sugar bowls. She'd take clothes and she'd give you them for the clothes. It was like a swap and I remember my mother giving her, she had a green coat with a black astrakhan collar and hadn't she got it on her the next time she called, well I went ballistic, I kept telling her she stole my mother's coat. I said, 'Why did you steal my mother's coat, I want it back.' 'Your mother got her dishes for that,' and I said 'No she didn't.' I was very cheeky, I was very upset and of course me mother killed me then. She had given the coat and the woman had given her saucers or whatever she had given her, but like little things like that stick in your mind. I'd say she was in her late fifties, it would be hard to tell, you wouldn't know what age they were then, I mean, look, we're fifty-eight, and women when I was a child that were fifty-eight looked one hundred and eight. We thought they were ancient and they did have hard lives.

Running Battle on Francis Street

At any stage during the day in Francis Street there was always Guinness dray delivering to the five shops and the Guinness's men in them days they always seemed as if they were big men. Guinness's men used to supply wearing big coats with belts and they always looked like big men and you can imagine the scene that there would be, four or five pony and carts with hops steaming out of them. These belonged to farmers from Tallaght who bought the hops to feed cattle and pigs. The farmers always had a pint or two before they drove the pony and cart home to Tallaght. Guinness's men and the milk men would be there too. Then all of a sudden Bang Bang would arrive. Bang Bang was a local character who carried this huge key in his hand but he used to hold his key as if it was a gun. Now, imagine grown men who lived through the era of cowboy films – when Bang Bang would arrive on the scene there would be a shooting scene and you'd have the Guinness's men hiding behind their barrels and hiding behind their horses and Bang Bang would be in the doorway, he'd be shooting at them and they'd be shooting back. All of these adult men would take part in a mock gun battle in Francis Street and you can imagine like, three horses with steaming hops coming out of them, a big large horse pulling big large Guinness's dray with gallons and gallons of Guinness on them and these big men having a running battle with Bang Bang. Unbelievable, but it was a fantastic place to grow up in. All human life was there.

Bang Bang. Photo courtesy of the Freer family.

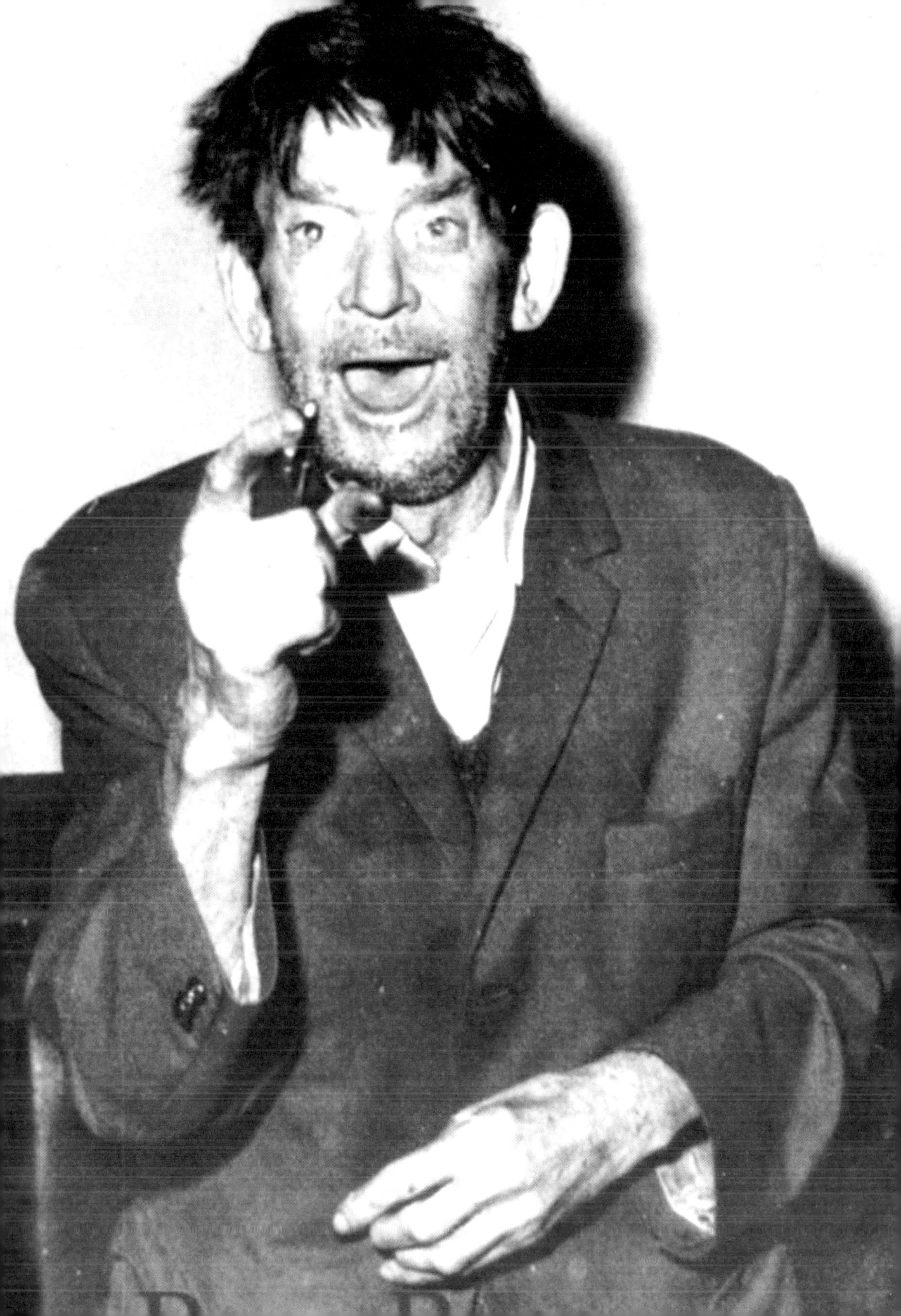

68/158 Boys School

I liked school but I wasn't very attentive. When I was a kid I was always drawing. I used to like drawing boats and aeroplanes and trains. I was a devil for this and I got more clouts over drawing than anything else. That teacher used to murder me for drawing. One day I was walking out to the toilet. I was in one class, me younger brother, was in another and the teacher Mr. B – he had me brother bent over the table and d'ye know the big pointers they used to use on maps like a snooker cue, he was beating me brother on the backside with that. I was only just gone eleven then and I ran in and said, 'Excuse me what are you doing?' He said, 'It's nothing got to do with you.' I said, 'Excuse me what do you mean it has nothing to do with me, that's my brother and you're beating the shite out of him.' 'Well,' he said, 'he didn't do his exercise last night.' 'Well,' I said, 'you don't punish a fella for not doing his exercise. You keep him back and you make him do it in front of you. That's what you do.' 'Are you telling me how to do me job?' he said, 'No sir, I'm not trying to tell you how to do your job. I'm just asking you in a nice way not to hit me brother.' I said, 'I'll tell you one thing that if I catch you hitting me brother I'll take your life' and d'ye know what he said? 'You'll never be anything in life,' he says, 'D'ye know what you'll do,' he says, 'you'll end up working in the Corporation on the roads.' That's as true as my Mam's in heaven.

69/158 Miraculous Medal and Sodalities

It was lucky you stayed with religion; it was beat into you. In the home you had to go to Miraculous Medal on a Friday and a Monday and then you had your Sodality on a Sunday. The Sodality – a group of children would go. You would go to confession and a lecture and then you'd get Mass the following day and another lecture. The Miraculous Medal was on a Monday. That was devotions to Our Lady. You said the prayer on a Monday, Friday you had the Sacred Heart, the day of the Sacred Heart. They used to have the seven weeks we used to have for Lent, what were they called, the Retreats – they were horrific. They'd be held in the Parish Church every night and . . . My God some of those priests should have been shot – every night of the week the whole of Lent. I think you just got Mass on Sunday. At the retreat, you'd go and you'd listen to him give you orders, fire and brimstone and tell you

1950s

Kitty Hatton. Photo courtesy of Eddie Hatton.

about hell and the sins and everything you did was a sin. We were sixteen and seventeen and you had to go to them. In confession the priest would be asking me about going with a boy and were you 'passionate'? Jesus, Mary and Joseph we didn't even know what passion was! 'Did he touch you anywhere?' 'Well he kind of put his hand there…' 'Where?' You'd think we were having sex in the middle of the road! It's no wonder there were so many old maids around this area 'cos people were afraid of your life. Jesus if you were pregnant those days and not married – It was disgraceful.

Inhibition

We had awful inhibitions about our bodies and that is for sure and well in those days you weren't to get pleasure and if you did get a little bit you'd be saying, 'Jesus I have to go to confession.' I mean, live and let live. Priests – I don't agree with them flying around every night with different partners, that's their business. I couldn't care less, but with us it was the total opposite, like you were afraid to fall in love with anybody you know.

Some of them got married early and some of them got married late; there was a variety. It was common for very young marriages, eighteen or nineteen; a lot thought they'd never get out of the house. A lot did. A lot got married for that reason, they just got married to get out of the house and then God help them. I remember a girl got married in Patrick Street, she'd be forty or forty-two or even more, she was pregnant. They were a lovely couple and she was pregnant. They had to go up to the priest. She had to be married on the side altar at six o'clock in the evening and she had to wear blue. She wasn't allowed wear white but that stuck in my head and I was only about twelve and I thought it was the most cruel thing that could have happened to anybody. You went early in the morning, you couldn't be married on the main altar, that wasn't heard of.

Hoolie

Me Ma was pregnant on me when she came over to the Ross Road and I was the first to be born in the house and being the first girl after six boys, me granny said, 'Ah there's another Biddy Butter, go down and spend the rent money.' And they had a hoolie in, me Ma was in the back bedroom, this is what me Ma said. Every Sunday night on the road they'd have a hoolie, just

1950s

one a week, and somebody's windows would go in. We were kids, we would be watching – the pubs closed at 8 o'clock and somebody would bring home a pack with a few bottles and they'd have a party and a sing-a-long and the whole lot. We'd be listening to the records and the whole lot.

They used to have turns I think, they used to have turns in bringing them up to the house, right, and we would be all put into bed and all the oul fellas and the women, you know, the neighbours of the road would be brought up and gave a sup of beer or whatever and they'd start their singsong and they'd have a sandwich and a little hoolie. There might be singing and put the oul, what do you call it, the gramophone on and one of us would be called out of the room to turn the thing on and listen to 78s, what's his name? Dean Martin. And they'd be all dancing and singing and all, clapping their feet and the whole lot. I'd be thinking it was great and then me brother would say, 'Dad I want to go to the toilet.' 'Just go out and go to the toilet' and the bottles would be put down on the floor and he would only be about five or six and he'd be drinking out of the bottles.

John Freer and his sister Margaret Freer. Photo courtesy of the Freer family.

The Emigrant

There was absolutely nothing in Dublin at that time in the 1950s. Unemployment for youths of sixteen to seventeen was anywhere from sixty to seventy per cent. I went to England for a year.

One day the landlady told me there were two CID men at the door looking for me, I was supposed to join the army. I was supposed to get drafted into the army. So she said they said they would be back tomorrow, I was gone on the boat that night to Dublin.

Then I got the call from my Aunt asking if I wanted to come out to New York and I took her up on it. I didn't really want to come out but at that time Dublin was, I mean there was absolutely nothing, no chance of work. I mean for my age I'd say it was sixty per cent unemployment at that time. There was nothing. Then I got the call from my Aunt asking if I wanted to come out to New York and I took her up on it. So I ended up coming out then. I went to America, I stayed with my Aunt Bridie for about eight months and then I got drafted into the United States Army, which I didn't mind. I didn't mind that. I didn't want to be in the English Army. The U.S. I didn't mind but just the English Army didn't run well with me.

I haven't looked back since. Best thing I ever done. I live very comfortably, I raised a wonderful family. I wouldn't have got that in Dublin. At that time I hadn't a trade, didn't even have a primary, left school at thirteen. Being second eldest of a large family you needed money to live. There's only two left from when I was growing up as a kid. They made out okay. A lot of them emigrated too – Australia and Canada. A lot of them emigrated.

"The pub was Corbetts in Werburgh Street. Included in the photo is Albert Norton, Georgie Cleary, Jackie Kenny, Richie Byrne, Jack Doran, Morris Power, Patsy Dalton, Tom Dalton, John Hughes, Billier Connerton and me dad Andrew Kerfoot. The photo was taken in late 50s early 60s, I don't know who took the photo, me dad always had it and has passed away so I be guessing the barman took the photo". Photo and caption courtesy of Andrew Kerfoot.

19

High Street, 1968. Copyright: Dublin City Public Libraries.

Considerable changes have taken place on this street. All the buildings to the left have been demolished. The road has been widened to three times the width shown. The factories in the background have been replaced by a hotel and an apartment block.

60s

HENSHAW'S
CHRISTCHURCH PLACE, DUBLIN.

We carry extensive stocks of:
GENERAL IRONMONGERY, IRON AND STEEL, SEEDS, CHINA AND GLASS.

Stockists for the Famous 'ESSE' Cooker.   *A visit will repay you.*

Advertisement in the Capuchin Annual, 1936. Image courtesy of Chris Reid.

73/158 Horses and Henshaw's

Then the Guinness horses used to be parked outside her door. Molly's husband worked in Guinness's. And he parked the horse and car on the Ross Road and we'd be all sitting on the horse and car, he'd give us a shot around the block and bring us back. Brick Byrne was his name. He was a good old sport. The horse and cars then, it was always the horse and cars then. Henshaw's (Henner's) had the horse and cars coming out on to the Ross Road, you'd be scutting them, I used to scut them down the road and up the road; we'd have a bit of a laugh, right. We'd jump on the back of them and hold on, and if your Da or if Moggy seen you, 'Get off that feckin' horse and car!' That's the way she was minding us, she was always around us, right, but she looked out for us, and I have to say she was a lovely woman. You'd say, 'Did you get new teeth Moggy? You're able to open your mouth now wider,' you know, the kids would be shouting up to her, but she'd say, 'I'll give you a good crack on the arse,' she'd say to them, you know.

74/158 Nancy on The Ross Road

There was Nancy on the Ross Road, she used to feed the horses; the horses would be all queuing up to go in to Henshaw's and she'd take the head of cabbage out and start feeding them. Nancy, she used to live there in number 9, 9D Ross Road, her and her two brothers. They were real old, real gentle people and if she seen a dog or anything she'd feed it, she was a lovely woman. She was still alive when I got married, in 1973. I'd say she died in about '86,

....1960s

she died before my Ma. Henshaw's, that was a lovely big, huge shop in the front of Christchurch. It was like a department store, it was like Switzer's. We weren't allowed in to it though I did go in. I was never upstairs in it, but I remember one day me Ma walked me around it, there was only me and me Ma and she brought me around to let me have a look at all the lovely delft china, everything like that, all lovely things in it, gorgeous. I do always say when I look at it now isn't it a waste, there's nothing there (see page 210).

And you always knew the tourists coming down, the tourists was never touched, not like now, they're going along and they're reefing the bags off them, and where are they reefing only at Christchurch. Years ago them people could walk around, sail down the Ross Road, stand at the railings and look at the kids playing in the yard and probably say hello to Moggy, and Moggy'd say, 'There you are, I hope you're having a nice time.'

Names and Premises Remembered

$\frac{75}{158}$

When you walk across from Jurys as if you're going up in to High Street, there was a kind of a clinic there, I don't know what they called it (the Bad Health Clinic), it was probably asthma or TB or whatever, I remember the shops, the little dairy shop beside Henshaw's and then there was another little shop use to do tobacco and something else and then there was the pub and then next to the pub then there was another little sweet shop. Then there was Mrs. Johnson's shop (see page 138) and then there was the Ray's and Johnnie's right up to the next shop and they were all shops, sweet shops, tobacco shops and then there was the park and then at the park gates there was a pub, there was a garage, there was another pub, that brought you in to Kevin Street. I remember on the opposite side on Lord Edward Street you had the Castle Inn, the bed shop (Richardson's), the Pie factory, the sewing factory, and there was a sewing factory up over Christchurch as well, then there was the church, then there was a lodging house, then there was a pub, then there was Ship Street, there was a coal shop there and then on Bride Street there was O'Beirne's pub, McColgan's pub, McHugh's pub, that was up, Finnegan's and Kenny's (see photo on next page), then it came up to, up to all the rag stores, you know the rag stores (Woolfson's) where you brought the rags up and you got probably three pence for a bag of rags on Bride Street, then you had Jacob's all that block, and that was it . . . I think?

'Kenny's Corner' public house was on the corner of Golden Lane and Bride Street. Golden Lane was widened and residential housing, known as 'Gulliver's Flats', were built (early 1990s), replacing the buildings visible in the photo located on Golden Lane. Photo by Elinor Wiltshire. Courtesy of The National Library of Ireland.

$\frac{76}{158}$ Babies and Prams

When people had babies and prams, and they'd be down on the road, people that lived around there, you could put your baby outside anyone's window, and knock at the window and say, 'I'm putting the baby there.' 'Yea, it's alright, I'll throw me eye on it.' The neighbours was great, and you wanted for nothing, and they always knocked at your door to see were you alright, and you always got a message for them. There was loads of other neighbours like across the road that you would say, they were good neighbours too, everyone was kind of, everyone was good neighbours on the Ross Road, it was a nice place.

Hercules and The Invalidity Milk

My Ma'd go up to the Mills in Thomas Street, that's where the Vicar street is, it's a chemist, right. Then she got that she used to just go to the Market when she'd be rushing. The Iveagh Market, you could get food there. Mr. Flanagan was there, where she'd get her groceries. She'd get her meat off Mr. Flynn. They'd be in the Iveagh, one facing the other, right. And of course then she'd give you the pram to bring home and she'd be in the wash house washing, right, or then she used to run a bill in the shops, the shops around the corner used to run the bills, right, and say she need bread or milk during the week, we always got the milk – the invalidity milk, me Ma used to get for me and me brother. He was only born a pound, the size of him now, he's like Hercules.

The way you collected your few bob off the neighbours was you went and got their milk every morning before you went to school and they'd give you a shilling at the end of the week. You might have ten shillings and you bought your baby stuff and you'd give a few bob to your Ma and you had your picture money out of it.

John Freer at the Carmelite Wrestlng Club in 1966. Photo courtesy of the Freer family.

78/158 I'd Get The Turf . . .

From the Turf Depot down in Kevin Street, before I went to school, meself and me younger brother, one of the younger ones, would go with me, and we had an auld pram or a trolley that you made yourself. We were up at half seven in the morning doing that down in the Turf Depot, queuing to get your turf, you know. It would be a long queue, it was a hundred-weight of turf, there was a docket for it, given out by the Corporation. These auld countrymen, who probably stayed in the Iveagh Hostel, you know, filling the bags, in the middle of winter, you know, you'd be tying the bags with bits of string and your hands would be so cold, you know. So I'd get the turf, and I'd bring them up to the women, and you'd get one-and-six or two-shillings, but, I know I'm big now, but I was smaller, what I used to do, meself and me brother would pull the four stone up the first flight of steps in the flats, then I'd sit on the top step, and we'd hooch it up onto me back, then I'd be able to carry it up. That was four stone. So there was two bags which made a hundred-weight, eight stone. So I was small enough then, you know, but I could lift, you know, we'd do two of them before we went to school.

But there was one particular woman, and as I said, my mother died when I was thirteen, so she was hardly alive when I did that, but one woman used to get a couple of dockets, I don't know how she did it, but instead of paying me, she'd give me a docket, so I brought home the hundred-weight of turf to me mother. I mean a hundred-weight of turf was better than two shillings.

79/158 Chopping and Selling Sticks

When you were not in school, you were doing some work, you'd be doing something, I used to chop sticks and sell them. We didn't get pocket money. I used to chop sticks, and go round and sell them, and I think, you got, a shilling. There was always wood, there was always derelict buildings around, and we would bring home wood and bits of stuff in a bag to put on the fire. You'd chop up the sticks and you'd get the old bicycle tubes, everybody had bikes, you'd cut up a bicycle tube with the scissors it would be like a piece of elastic and wrap a bundle of the wood. It was handy to keep the sticks together in bundles. There was a guy down at the end of the Ross Road, I forget his name (John Dalton), he was a couple of years older than me, he used to chop sticks as well, but he used to get elastic bands somewhere, obviously

John Dalton chopping wood in the yard at the rear of the flats on Bride Street and The Ross Road. Photo courtesy of the Freer family.

he bought them, I didn't know where you would buy them. I thought that was the height of progress! That was very forward-thinking in them days! And me with the bicycle tube, which did the same job – mind you that was a nice bit of recycling! We recycled everything – there was a use for everything.

And then down at the shops of course, your man, the shop keeper, had the bill as well, you know, everything was on tick, the mother would send you down to the shop to get something, and they'd put it in the book. That was normal for us.

Ma's Teeth

I went to school, I used to bring all me brothers to school and when I'd bring them to school, some of them would walk out the other door and they'd go on the mitch and they'd be missing, right, and at that time we didn't have a sense of time to come home at such and such a time and if you weren't home your father or mother knew you were mitching. My Ma was only after getting her teeth out after the last baby, all her teeth out and she got new teeth – false teeth. And she used to put them in the jam jar at night. I thought it was horrible, I thought they were horses teeth they were giving people, right, so my youngest sister was in the class with me and Ma knocked at the door and she said, 'I want to see me children, me teeth is missing' to the teacher, right. And when we came out me Ma had no teeth and she said, 'What did you do with me teeth?' and I said 'I haven't got your teeth ma.' , 'I haven't got your teeth ma, Jesus! I didn't take your teeth.' 'Well one of you took the teeth.' So Mary, that's me younger sister, she came out and me Ma asks her, 'Where's me teeth Mary?' and she tries to say something but can't. 'What's wrong with you? What's in your mouth?' me Ma says. The false teeth were stuck in Mary's mouth! She couldn't get them out, we had to bring her down to the toilet and try and reef them out. She brought them to school and put them in her mouth and went quack, quack, quack with the teeth. And the teeth were too big and they were caught in her own teeth. That was around 1960.

Wake

My mother, Agnes Travers, died at home in 1964. The sun was shining that morning and me mother said to me 'Can I have a cup of tea? Oh that's a lovely sup of tea.' I turned around and poured it. Me sister next door. I knocked on the wall for me sister and she came in and I said there's something wrong with me mother. She said me mother's gone. Lovely death. We had the wake for me mother. We didn't have to invite them, the neighbours came and they sat up with us all night with me mama. I sat up all night with her and you had to have a good sup of drink because when the neighbours came you had to give them a drink before they went home. People would make you sandwiches and sit up all night. Most of the people when they come in you'd ask them what they'd have – a bottle of stout? When it came to the night time before she went to the chapel we were sitting up all night with her and the next night she was going to church. She never went to a funeral parlour. 'When I'm dead,' she

.... 1960s

said, 'make sure you respect all my friends.' That was her wishes. Me and me two sisters and me brothers got in plenty of drink, got in plenty of whiskey and six or seven people sat with us all night. Me mother was in the coffin. Oh you'd be all talking about the old times. I got a woman in to wash me mother and put the habit on her. Now they don't put habits on them, they dress them in their ordinary clothes, but that time you put a habit on them and she laid her out, put sheets around her and a crucifix on her. We done it in style but when a person died in a hospital you put a candle but if they died at home you put a wreath on the door and you had to get black bands and black ties. She went to the chapel next night. She was there all that night and the following night and the following morning she went to the church and then she went to Mount Jerome.

Two women at the entrance to High Street Church. Notice the low rise buildings which have long since been demolished. Courtesy of The National Library of Ireland. Photo by Elinor Wiltshire.

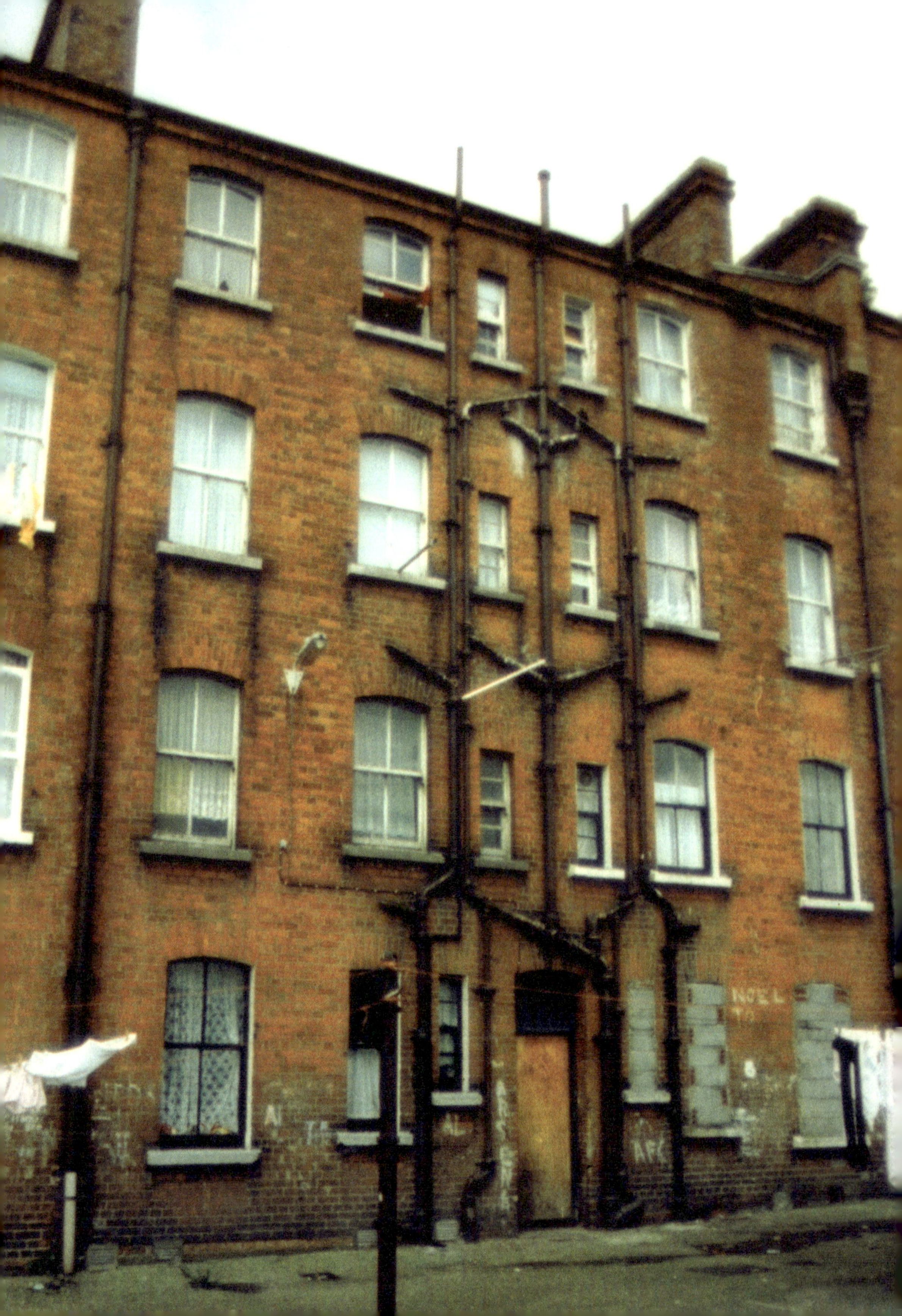
NOEL
AFC

.... 1960s

82/158 Climbing The Pipes

When I was a child I used to get into the flat by climbing up the pipes out the back. All the pipes used to be on the outside of the buildings then. Nicholas Street is four stories high and for a few years I was well able to climb to the top of the building using the pipes. There wasn't many would climb them you know, unless they were breaking into a flat maybe, but there wouldn't be many even then would climb up the whole four stories. Seventy or eighty feet up. Occasionally women would accidentally lock themselves out of their flats, I'm thinking of one woman in particular here, and it was one of the women who lived on the top floor, and she of course knew me and saw me climb the pipes before and I was always around you see, and she asked me to help her. She told me she had locked herself out, and she asked me to climb up and get into her flat through the back and open the door for her. I would have been about thirteen or fourteen and getting big. I hadn't climbed to the top floor in months but I climbed up, I was like a monkey, it was very easy for me and I'd get in through the toilet window. I had done this so many times, and I remember climbing up on this day, and just as I got up to the top floor some of the rivets were torn out from the wall. The pipe came out from the wall, and I fuckin' froze – it was only another couple of feet up, and I'd get holds of the window sill. I climbed the last few feet, pulled the catch on the window, got in, and opened the door for her. She gave me a couple of shillings, then it was down to the sweet shop to spend some of it. But that was the last time I did it.

83/158 A Sad End to a Dance

I'd buy the best. Very modern. Like something similar like what's in today you know the tight skirts, lovely jackets, fitted blouses and jumpers, shoes – twinsets. The early sixties and I was very fashion conscious then and I'd be very careful of them. We used to go to Palm Beach and the Arcadia, the Barracks in Kevin Street. The Barracks – it's in the police station. They used to have a dance of a Saturday night. The Guards they ran it really so everyone had to be right going in, so you couldn't be drunk. I was actually there the night Kennedy was assassinated. I was in the Barracks that night. It was announced. I was in total shock, total devastation because he'd only visited that year, I think and the cavalcade came up to City Hall and I remember being in Parliament Street and I thought he was only gorgeous. I was only

The yards at the back of the flats, circa 1980s. The exterior pipes can be seen clearly here. Photo courtesy of Kieran Kavanagh, Dublin City Architects Division.

fifteen I was, he must have been coming from the park and I think he was going to the Castle and he was bronze, tanned, I mean no-one had a tan in Ireland in those days d'you know what I mean, he was gorgeous. Everyone was so excited and then he was assassinated – everyone was devastated. They stopped the dance and everyone went home.

84/158 We Shouldn't Have Jeered Her

There was this woman and she was a nurse and she married this man but he was very abusive to her, he was very fond of his drink and she said, 'Well if I can't beat you, I'll join you,' She was a nurse and she joined him and she ended up on the streets. Her name was Annie. We used to jeer her and she used to chase us, right, as kids. But she'd go up to your hall at night and have a sleep on the landing and one of the neighbours would come out with a bottle of tea, a glass bottle of tea and a sandwich for her. She just got fed up of life; her kids were taken off her. I think she had three kids. But I don't remember the kids, I only remember her. We were told all this as we were growing up, you shouldn't have jeered that woman; that woman is a lovely woman you know, she was beautiful looking, ah she had lovely blonde hair like a film star.

85/158 School Days

We all left school when we were fourteen and we just couldn't wait to get out of it. Because of the beatings you were getting in school, you know. And corporal punishment was rife and it was open season and it wasn't just a stick. In my school one teacher had the leg of a chair and another teacher had half of a snooker queue. Another used a pole that was meant to be used for opening the windows, and punch you with the fist; I mean anything. It was open season.

I wrote my first poem when I was ten and we were in school and we had to write a poem about snow. And I always found it easy to put words together and I brought the poem up to the teacher and he read it and I got a clatter to the side of the head. And he said now go back down there and get me the book that you copied that poem out of. I said I didn't copy it I wrote it myself and then I got another clatter. And he searched my bag and the desk and the whole lot and then he brought me down to the headmaster. Same response from him and, 'Where is the book, you didn't write that.' And here you go and, 'If I couldn't write that poem then you couldn't write it' and then he brought down the parish priest. This is true. You will go to hell for telling lies and I said, 'I wrote that poem myself.' And then he says to me you couldn't have wrote that poem because you couldn't spell those words. So this was a class and they were looking at people from tenements and the flats and all that. So that turned me off poetry. But I have written seventeen poems in the last two years. Poetry—it's in you and a true poet will write from what he feels.

"We couldn't wait to get out of school because of the beatings we got. Corporal punishment. It was open season. It wasn't just the stick. In my school one teacher used the leg of a chair. Another had half a snooker cue. Another used a pole for opening windows." [11]

Study

I preferred to be out playing with everyone else a lot of the time, but as I got older, you know, a teenager, I dropped all that. Started concentrating a bit more and getting more into school. It was neglected before, now I realised I wouldn't get anywhere if I didn't, and I didn't want to hang around the streets. I could study in the house. And school as well. I didn't see the advantage of hanging around the streets. I did a bit of that all right but I got tired of it. The same old places.

Me Father's Footsteps

I was a young chap, twelve or thirteen, then I started working on a messenger bike for a lovely Lady called Mrs. Mooney. I got to know the people very well and they all liked me, and I was making a lot of money for that time. It was 1962, my wage at that time was three pound ten shilling a week but after getting to know the people over the months and coming into years you get one guy giving you a pound for doing the messages and another lady would give you ten shillings, a half-a-crown here, and five shillings. I know it helped my Mam out because me dad didn't work at that time. He was on what you call relief work for the Corporation. They took him on for a couple of weeks and when it got slack they left him off and then they sent for him again. That went on for years 'til eventually he went permanent with them. It's hard to believe he's seven years dead. He was thirty-nine years in the place. I'm just gone thirty years in the place. People laugh at me; it's a long time 30 years in the one job. I got a wonderful opportunity when I was only fourteen and I blew it. It was the sorriest thing I ever did. The lady I worked for, her daughter's husband, Jack was his name, a fine big handsome man. He retired recently, he was a commandant in the army and way back then he asked me did I want a golden opportunity. I answered that I didn't know what he was speaking about. 'Well I'll put it to you in your language,' he says, 'If I got you a job in the army,' he says, 'the army would be paying you to keep yourself clean and keep yourself fit and just be on the job on request,' he said, 'I promise you very faithfully if you do what I say you'll go places.' However, at that time, I was hearing stories from different friends of mine who lost fathers and brothers in the war and these stories stayed in my head. I told Jack that I'm not going to go into the army. I decided I would try and follow in me father's footsteps. I went into the Corpo in 1973. The poor father was in the Corpo thirty-nine years and was only out five years when he passed away.

Saved From The Industrial Schools

I seen like kids from my years being put into Black Marias and being driven to Artane. He would have been about eleven and he is dead now actually. The school inspector went out of his way to get as many kids as possible to Artane and I know that for a fact. And now that day I was mitching from school – now we wanted to learn. We didn't mitch from school because we hated school,

.... 1960s

we mitched because we didn't have the money for the books and we were beaten with sticks and that, you know. And if you look back now, how can it be your fault if you don't have the money for your school books if you are nine or ten years of age. You know, I was mitching for six weeks and I was brought to court that day and so was this young lad. And me grandmother came over with me, granny the dealer, and she got hold of the school inspector outside the court. And she told him, she got him by the tie and it got to the stage where I didn't know the difference between his tongue and his tie. She had him by the neck and when we got to the court that day the inspector said that I had never been in trouble or anything like that. But neither had the other fella you see. He was in the same class yet the inspector spoke up for me and maybe because he had heard about me and he knew what would have happened outside the court. My grandmother stood there with her hat pin. The women in those days they always dressed in black and me grandmother always woke black. Black shawls and black hats and black rounded hat and a pearl stuck in it with a pin that was about six inches long you know. And that was their weapon you know, the grandmothers, and they would use it too. But I remember the other young fella being dragged screaming by policemen and his mother trying to get him away. He wasn't too bad till his mother started crying, you know, and that upset him. It will never leave my mind.

Artane Industrial School. Photo courtesy of the Christian Brothers Province Centre.

1960s ....

$\frac{89}{158}$ Daingean

My brother Joe let out on me one day and told me things what happened; ah he told me this very sad story. It's only lately now he's been talking, now he's able to get it out of him. He says to me, 'You know what, one of your grandsons is very like a little young fella that was in Daingean with me.' Joe was, what, thirteen then. He said 'there was about 16 boys in a dormitory and this little boy's mother was after dying and he was put into Daingean. We never knew what the young fella used to be taken out of the bed at for night time, right. Like one or two of the Christian Brothers got tough with me but I'd get tough back with them, right. So here this night the little boy was crying and he says to me, you know what, he says, you get into my bed and I'll get into your bed, the young fella wouldn't talk about what was happening'. So here, so they swapped beds, the young fella was only eight or nine years of age, they swapped bed and there was a new Christian Brother was brought down to take the young fella out of the bed and when he took the young fella and dragged him down to where they do drag them to they discovered it was me brother Joe. They gave me brother an awful hiding, right, he was in hospital for two weeks before me Ma knew. Then they put him out breaking the stones to make the roadway. When he was put back into the dormitory the little boy was never found and he always swore that child was killed. He said them brothers were abusing everybody down there, do you know what I mean? It still plays on his mind.

Daingean Reformatory. Photo courtesy of Offaly Historical & Archaeological Society.

Altar Boys

I was an altar boy, all of us were altar boys, meself and me brothers. Well as the mouse said to the trap, 'We won't go into that,' because the abuse thing raised it's ugly head there, there was a bit of that went on there. That's been documented elsewhere and I don't think I can go into it here.

The churches were always full then. I served Mass in High Street Church, I don't know how many masses there was, but there was certainly four or five on a Sunday morning, and the half twelve Mass was huge, the way the Poles have their Mass in High Street now. I served Mass in Back Lane with the Hostel. That was a sad auld place. Homeless men. I used to serve Mass on a Sunday morning. I used to get a shilling from the man who ran the place, and I could still smell the bodies in the church. A lovely little church. It would hold about seventy or eighty men and they had to go to Mass, they had no choice, then they got their breakfast. I never really saw them, because I used to get me breakfast served to me then, on me own. I'd get a big fry, rashers and sausages and eggs, sure that was grand, sure I didn't get that at home!

In Easter 1966, when the Latin Mass finished I read out the lesson in High Street Church in English, and that was the first time it was done, I believe. So standing up in front of the whole, at midnight Mass, and the church packed I read the lesson. That was Easter 1966, and I was twelve

Altar boys leading a Corpus Christi procession. Photo by Elinor Wiltshire, courtesy of The National Library of Ireland.

1960s

The Rat and The Nun

I remember that yard used to be walking with rats, the rats was huge, big huge things. There was a story that stands out, and I remember like I'd go into Mrs. Forte's, or they'd come in to us, one or the other, so our doors was kind of always open, and I remember I was in their house, and I was sitting on a stool or something, and me Ma and Da was there, and somebody says, 'Don't turn around, Marion, don't turn around,' but I didn't know what they meant. But it seems the rat was after coming up the stairs, now from the bottom, the back door was open, and it came right up the very top, it came right up, and it came in to our house. I turned around, and when I turned around the rat ran out, and ran into the woman next door, because her door was open, and I'll never forget it, the woman had a piano, she always had a piano, and she had a doll, it was about that size, do you remember they were out, you know, a nun, a doll dressed up as a nun, an old-fashioned doll, it was a nun. They used have it dressed up in all sorts of different costumes for it but this one was a nun, and I'll never forget it, and the rat ran up the nun's

Pedestrians on O'Connell Street, 1960s. Photo courtesy of The National Library of Ireland.

skirt, and it was running around the house, but you'd think it was the nun running! I'll never forget it, and all the men ran up, and they were all beating the thing and they killed it in the end.

92/158 Hoppers

You went down to Myra Hall in Francis Street and you got checked for head lice and fleas – hoppers they were called. It was rampant in the 60s in Dublin and you got deloused, as they called it. You know, DDT. They put something in your hair and that. I don't know where they came from – the hoppers – people used to say the turf. Or other people used to say the mattresses. They used to have mattresses with the horse hair in them, you know. And I remember standing outside the chemist one day when I was about eight or nine years or age and a woman said to me can you go in there son and get me a drum of DDT. They would be too embarrassed to go in and ask for it. I always remember that and I mean you didn't want anyone to know that you had hoppers, you know. But we all had them and the place was walking with them. And our mothers used to get a fine comb and hold your head over a newspaper, and reef the head off you with the comb and they would be all falling out on the paper. And then into the fire and bang, bang, they would crackle. The fleas – the hoppers – lived in the mattresses and you would wake in the morning and you would have all red spots on you where they would bite you. I remember years ago at a funeral talking to some people about the flats and going back to the tenements and everyone in the pub they started scratching themselves, talking about hoppers and you know it brought it back to you.

93/158 The Wringer

You carried your washing up to the laundry up by the Iveagh Market and washed it in the basins, put it into a boiler, put it in the rinser and then brought it up the wringer. Then you put the clothes in the wringer, you put it on the big steel horse to dry them. I've done the wash house with me ma. I did the washing for me Ma like, I'd go up, like my Ma was always a very nervous person, there was always bullies there, bullies like. If my Ma was putting the washing into the spinner she'd be after dragging the bath up, the iron bath and putting it into the spinner and the man would turn it on and me Ma would go back down to do another load. And another woman would come up and say clothes in the wringer right, so my Ma wasn't getting the clothes dry enough. She'd say, 'Clothes in the Wringer' and she'd be after opening it. She would take the clothes out and put her own stuff in. She'd throw them down and put her own in, so there was about three women like that in the wash house and my Ma would be sweating, the sweat would be pouring off her and it was just after the last baby and I said I'll go up ma, I'll bring the washing up for you. The woman knew me Ma and liked me Ma and the whole lot and she'd say go to number six basin. There was a big steel thing you pulled out, it was the size of the room and you put all the clothes on it, iron bars, right. So here I come along and I'd go up and then me Ma, one day I went in and I seen me Ma washing and she was putting the clothes in the wringer and I stood back and I watched and I seen this one coming along and taking the clothes and just throwing them on the ground. I was angry for her, looking at your Ma getting tormented like that. Me Ma came from a respectable family and so did me Da. She had loads of work to do then this was all happening. I said, 'I'll go up Ma and I'll do the washing.' 'No you won't you'll get me into trouble, them people passing in the street will say something to me.' 'Ma, did you ever learn how to say fuck off?' and she'd say, 'God bless us don't be saying them things, I wouldn't, I wouldn't say that to anybody.'

94/158 The Rag Man

The rag man would come around, 'Rags! rags! rags!' he'd shout. He stopped around the... I'd say I must have been about 18, '68 I'd say, '67. He was a fella on a horse and cart. He'd have goldfish in little jars. He would give you them if you bought down a good overcoat. Give you gold fish, sure there were many old things belonging to me Da, I gave him me Da's shoes and he'd be looking for them. 'I don't know what's after happening to them Da,' and of course then he'd lose the head, he'd lose the head with you. And the rag man always came of a Friday. Friday or Saturday morning, right, when he'd know that your parents would be either out getting the messages either one day or the other and he'd come of a Tuesday as well because he'd know that the women would be up washing their clothes in the wash house that was up beside the Iveagh Market.

Bronze Plaque installed on Ross Road. Story no. 94/158. See no. 12 on page 8 and 9. Photo by Chris Reid.

'Rags, rags, rags', he'd shout. The Ragman was a fella on a horse and cart, he'd have goldfish in little jars. He'd give you one if you brought down a good clover coat or some other article. Sometimes me Da noticed things missing and he'd lose the head. The Ragman always came of a Friday or Saturday morning - right, when he'd know your parents would be working or out getting messages. He'd come of a Tuesday as well because he'd know the women would be up washing their clothes in the wash house by the Iveagh market. He stopped coming around in 1967.

1960s

95/158 Heirlooms

Many years later we often said, 'My God we should have held on to it,' you know, it was good, the collectors would go mad for the stuff that we just gave away to dealers and everything, just, you know, they were coming up saying, 'I'll give you so much for that' and people were so glad to get the money they just let it go, and it would cost thousands of pounds today. We'd a beautiful sideboard there, and it was really black mahogany. It had a press each end of it, and then there was three or four drawers, and there was brass handles on the drawers, and mahogany, the shine on it, you didn't even have to polish it, you used to have to just go over it with a cloth, and you'd nearly see your face in it, with the shine; it was a beautiful article. And of course meself and me sister, we used to want to get rid of it, and my mother used to say, 'You can do what you like with it, whatever is here, when I'm gone, but as long as I'm here, that's staying,' because that was me mother's. And of course when she died then, all the modern stuff came out, and we thought we had to be modern, it was stupidity really, and we got rid of it all.

Kids outside 1A Old Bride Street, 17th April, 1965. Clockwise from the right: Sheila Freer, Bernadette Murtagh, John Freer, Frankie Herbridge, Paddy Herbridge and Chrissie Freer who was peeping out the window. Photo courtesy of the Freer family.

Work, Song – Opportunities

It's only when I look back on me life now, I'd give anything to be young again. Back in late 1966 I worked in Donnelly's Meat Factory in Cork Street for a few months. I was only in me early twenties. There were more girls than fellas. The fellas used to do all the heavy work rolling the hams. The women used to pack all the sliced ham beef and corn beef. I was a devil when I was younger for singing and I'm working away doing me ham and on this day I started singing one of Nat King Cole's songs. You could've heard a pin drop! I finished and one of the lads ran over and give me a hug. He says he thinks I can sing and I should audition with him. Says I, 'What are you on about?' 'This is only a nixer for me,' he says, 'I only work here part-time, I have a band,' he says, 'We go around the country,' he says, 'I wouldn't lie to you.' 'My name is Philip and if you get the Herald tonight or the Press go to the entertainment page and you'll see me and the band.' He asked me to meet the band but I didn't and he left Donnelly's soon after. Me, I wasn't long following him, I was sacked, for what I don't know, maybe out of jealousy because I used to work on the factory floor with all the girls and they liked me. Anyway thirty five years later I went up to see the sister in Crumlin. She lives up that way. I was crossing the road with me bike and this man is coming out of the Crumlin Shopping Centre and he didn't know me but I don't know what it is about faces but I knew him. He had his hair long afro-style with curls on him and I'm looking at him getting into this big beautiful car. It was a Mercedes – a silver Mercedes. Then I remember – 'Philip!' I said, 'how's it going?' and he looked at me and says, 'Sorry but you have me at a disadvantage.' I didn't mention me name but said, 'Does Nat King Cole ring a bell?' 'Jaysus, I don't believe it!' he says, 'you're the young fella who worked in Donnelly's.' 'That's right,' I said, 'What are you doing here?' 'Ah nothing,' he says, 'putting some money in the bank.' We talk for a few minutes and he tells me about his life as a professional singer and about his band and how difficult it was and how it all paid off and how happy he is. 'We're mostly down the country now,' he says, 'but we get plenty of work.' I said, 'I really genuinely thought you were joking back then.' 'By Jaysus you're a very silly man,' he says, 'I remember you had a great voice!' In 1966 he gave me the opportunity to join the band and I refused and here we were thirty five years later.

1960s

⁹⁷⁄₁₅₈ Earning Money

The following year, I joined the FCA (now called Reserve Defence Force (RDF)). I joined for money. I was fourteen you had to be sixteen and I lied about me age to join. You turned up twice a week, for parade, Tuesday or Thursday and Sunday morning. Then you went for two weeks in the summer, full time, down to Gormanstown, or up to Donegal. You were paid for two weeks, plus you were paid for turning up for the rest of the year. The next year, 1969, I went on camp staff, for two months, in Gormanstown. I earned a full soldier's wage for those two months, and, you know, for someone who didn't have any money it meant a lot to me to be earning money.

Gormanstown FCA camp was beside what was Butlins holiday camp, out in Meath, it was a training camp. However the camp was near what used to be the main Dublin to Belfast Road. It was August 1969. In the middle of the night one night we were all got out of our beds. I was issued live ammunition and put on guard. Late that night, buses arrived in the camp. They were packed with people from the North. These people had no belongings – they were refugees. They were put up in some of the billets, or huts. The whole thing was chaotic and very tense. The children did a lot of crying. Someone said it was because the Red Cross uniform was dark blue and the children thought they were the B Specials. I was a fifteen year old, fifteen and a half and I shouldn't have been there with a gun and live ammunition.

I used to work in the officers' mess, in the kitchen, and you know some of the officers now would be very toffee-nosed, the best of food, whereas what the others got was basic. Now I was fed great, working in the officers' mess, but if you had a job in the there, that was different. I was there when the astronauts landed on the moon. I remember watching it on the television in the mess, that was a big event; I drank two pints as well! I think it was night time because I remember coming out, and looking up at the night sky then at the light at the end of the building, and the light seemed to be waving around a bit. I was drunk.

'The first earthmen on another planet – Neil Armstrong and Edwin Aldrin' – The Irish Times, July 21, 1969. Inset picture: 'Mr. and Mrs. Joseph McGrady from Ardoyne, Belfast, with their children, Ann, Margaret, Anthony and Jim at the Army Refugee Camp, Gormanstown.' – The Irish Times, December 1969,

Mr. and Mrs. Joseph McGrady, from Ardoyne, Belfast, with their children, Ann, Margaret, Anthony and Jim at the Army Refugee Camp, Gormanston.

19

70s

Entrance to Derby Square from Werburgh Street, 1969. M. Johnston's Newsagents at no. 14 Werburgh Street is also visible. Derby Square was demolished in the late 1980s and replaced in the 1990s by the entrance to the Jurys Hotel carpark. Photo by Elinor Wiltshire. Courtesy of the National Library of Ireland.

From the time I was born Moggy was there. I'd be swinging on the lamp post (or scutting the back of the coal lorry) and she'd be sitting there at the window her dog beside her, watching the kids and the people. She had six kids herself and she was left a young widow. She'd wash the dead or anything to earn a shilling to rear them and if she never had a shilling she was always in good form. She'd go around for a few glasses of stout at Corbetts and would come around singing.

98/158 Moggy

There was one woman, Moggy they used to call her, Mrs. Dalton was her name, but Moggy we used to call her, and she was a character, a gas woman, everyone loved her. There was six tenants up the hall, and she was in the middle of us, ah she was a character, she was. Every time you'd be coming up and down the stairs, she'd be there, and she'd be talking to you and all. She'd have like a smock on her, you know the smocks that they used to wear years ago with all the buttons up, and the two pockets, we kind of all wore them now as I think of it. It was a blue colour. There used to be a pub here where Jurys car park is, it used be called Corbett's, and she used to come around then, she'd come around at ten o'clock in the night, the woman, but she always made a few sandwiches, and she'd come around to have a glass of stout or something, but she'd always bring her sandwiches with her, to eat them. That's going back years now I'd say, that would have been before I even got married, but it was, it was a beautiful… you didn't want for anything. I'd say it was around the 1970s.

Ah I remember her from the time I was born she was there, she was there as long as I remember, she was a good sport. I could be swinging on the lamp post or scutting the back of the coal lorry and she'd be sitting there at the window her dog beside her watching the kids and the people or she'd come down and she'd probably sit on the step watching you, that's all they done, or went to the oul bingo when the bingo started in the Tivoli. Now Moggy would go around for a few glasses of Guinness and come around the street singing a song, we all listened to her, you know, we all learned all them songs. Children. She had six kids herself, there was Patrick, Harry and Maureen, Tom, Jimmy and John. And she was left a young widow to rear them you know. She'd wash the dead or anything to earn a shilling to rear them and if she never had a shilling she was always in good form. If Moggy was selling a suite of furniture she would send over to me Ma and she'd give me Ma the first preference of the suite of furniture, that was the first time we ever had a sofa. Me Ma bought it off Moggy and she was very good, very good to my Ma in any case, I'll always remember.

99/158 1 Ross Road - The Hall

Well on the bottom hall was Mrs. Byrne, she lived in 1A. Mrs. Byrne, that's what I was saying, her daughter and her son live underneath me now. She was a lovely woman too, and she had Mr. Byrne, was her husband, and there

Bronze Plaque installed on Ross Road. Story no. 98/158. See no. 18 on page 8 and 9.
Photo by Chris Reid.

was one thing, Mr. Byrne was a bricklayer, and he always had a fashion, when you'd come in, and you'd say 'good night Mr. Byrne' he always said, 'Goodnight, goodnight, goodnight,' he repeated himself three or four times, that's what we always remember about Mr. Byrne. The woman in the next door to her, Mrs. Kelly. She was a nice woman, quiet, came in and out, minded her own. And then when you'd come up the hall, there was Mrs. Dalton, well Mrs. Dalton was always standing out, and she'd give you a laugh and a joke, always, she was a character, everyone knew Moggy. Moggy, that was her nickname. And then next door to her was Mrs. Connaughton and she was lovely, and she was the woman that you'd see late of a Saturday night, scrubbing her steps, cleaning her steps. Then when you'd come up the steps, there was my mother lived there, and next door to her then was Mrs. Forte, and Mrs. Forte was our next door neighbour, and she was lovely.

100/158 A Babysitting Barman

I got a job working in Francis Street, the pub is just beside the Iveagh Market, as an apprentice barman, which was grand you know. The pub is still there but it's shut.

I would have been about nineteen or twenty, my boss used to live over the premises. He had two daughters, two little girls, and at the time they would have been about eight years of age and four years of age, and himself and his wife used to go out on a Wednesday night and I'd be in the pub downstairs, on me own, and I'd be expected to mind the kids! I was both babysitter and a barman and I'd be running up and down the stairs from six o'clock. The kids would be in the bedroom, two beds, and I'd run up the stairs to see if they were OK and they'd hear me coming, and they'd be jumping up and down, 'Pat, Pat, Pat' and I'd say, 'What? go asleep, go asleep' and I'd run back downstairs, and I'd run up again then down, then up and down, and eventually, by about nine, the two of them would be asleep. The door upstairs to the living accommodation wasn't locked. They were very different times – you could leave two young children, an eight year old and a four year old, upstairs, with an unlocked door, and leave a young man, who was meant to be doing a different job, to run up and down and keep an eye on them.

101/158 Discos and Showbands

I used to go to the school, St. Bridget's used to have a disco and I used to go to that. But when we started drinking I used to go down to Clogherhead. I remember me and Michael Byrne, we went to Clogherhead in Louth, we were only sixteen, and we used to bring two blankets and sleep in the barn, down the few drinks then, well more than a few but...

The Miami used to be on down there, I remember the Miami, Fran O'Brien wasn't it, Fran that was killed remember, the lead singer in the Miami. Remember Dickie Rock used to be with them and then another fella. But he was on down there at the time, it was great, the Aisling ballroom in Clogherhead. I would see them there and we used to drink in the pub called The Big Tree. Early 70s.

A newspaper advertisement for the Miami Showband. Image courtesy of Chris Reid.

102/158 Looking For a Job

I left school in 1970 at 14, you know, I went for interviews for jobs around that area when I moved up to St. Theresa Gardens. And quite a rough area as people thought on the outside. But the people that lived in it know it was a great place to grow up in and you would be doing OK in the interview till you gave them your address, you know, and then they'll say, 'We'll be in touch.' It happened like, it's not a chip that I have on my shoulder about it, it definitely happened. Like me and a lot of my friends around the flats joined the army. I was in the army for three years, unemployment was rife at certain stages in the 70s and it's going to happen again. And lots of my friends went off to

1970s

England and that, and my friend he is in the States. He is an electrician and he is over there.

103/158 Woolfson's Rag Stores

He would cut the rags and you just got loads of rags and put them into boxes and make them into shammies and all that. And you would put them in to the boxes and then they would weight the boxes. And they cut them and they weighed them at the side, and it would have to be bang on the weight. And they used to have horse hair and the weight of it and I used to have to drag it down the stairs. The weight of that horse hair is something else. And he sent me up to the loft there and said, 'That horse hair, can you bring it down.' And it weighed a ton and I couldn't hardly pull it and there were two of us bringing it down the stairs.

Iveagh Market, 1978. Copyright: Dublin City Public Libraries.

104/158 Washing Lines

We have little balconies now, and we put our washing out, but do you see the big yards out the back? Well we used to have our washing down there, and we used to all have to come down, and we'd have all lines then, and you'd hang out your washing there. The washing would be there all day, you know, and if it started to rain, somebody, a neighbour would be out getting in their washing, and they'd see your washing, and they'd call you, but while they'd be calling you, to tell you, they'd be taking in your washing for you, and if you don't answer them, they'd take in your washing for you, you could be out getting your messages or something, and they'd take in your washing, and when you'd come home, they'd have the washing in your house, do you know, they were, that's the type of neighbours they were, they were great neighbours. And they were always there to help you, and you knocked at one another's door, they weren't back biting, do you know what I'm trying to say – the neighbours was great, up the hall, the neighbours was fantastic.

We had to take our washing in. We had to take our washing in every Thursday. So anyone that moved in, we used to say to them, 'When you hang out your washing, take it in of a Thursday after dinner, because your washing will be gone.' Certain people who signed on at the Labour on Werburgh Street of a Thursday – they'd see the washing, and they'd take it on you, they'd come in and they'd rob all jeans.

105/158 Loitering, Cards, a Toss School

You could get locked up for loitering at the end of the road. The fellas used to play cards, the men. At the end of the Ross Road there. Where they used to play handball, just there. The men would play cards. They'd probably play rummy, and then there was a toss school of a Sunday in the yard. That was in our backyard and if you seen the cops coming you ran up and said 'Cops! Cops!', and you'd see them all running. And you'd often do it yourself just to run down and get the few bob off the ground and the cops would be coming up the yard and they'd say what are you doing, 'I'm hanging out the washing'. You'd always have a tea towel over your shoulder (see page 149).

1970s

$\frac{106}{158}$ Orphans

Both of them had come from orphanages as a lot of people from orphanages went into the army to get a bed and three meals. I did my training in Kilkenny. And they were both from the same orphanage in Wicklow somewhere. It was amazing how different they were. One fella never shut up talking and the other fella never spoke to anyone. But anyway this fella, Paddy was a few feet away beside my bed – he was the talker. And he would be screaming all night in his sleep and then when we would go to get our food, we didn't think it was great but he thought it was beautiful. Compared to what he used to get, you know, so. The quiet fella, he got married and that. But Paddy, he had nothing else and he had no family, you know, and he was really trying hard and I remember one day sticking up for him. And in those days you had to polish your own brass buttons and all that and he was always immaculate out in parade.

I went into the dining hall one morning and two big fellas were holding a knife to him and saying he was a rat and all that and a lick arse. And I hit one of them and I said, 'This is all he has and he is trying to make the best of it. He is not a rat, if he doesn't make it here, he is back on the streets.' That day he latched onto me, that day I stuck up for him in the dining hall and he used to follow me everywhere after that. Even though I was only 18, I was well over six foot at the time. And he used to follow me everywhere and he saw me as his protector and I wasn't a hard man or anything but one thing that I always hated in my life was bullying and all that type of shite.

Then I came across him a few times later in the 80s around Stephen's Green, he was drinking on the street and he asked me for money. I wouldn't give him money, I would buy him some food. Sometime later I went looking for him and the people that were with him said he died up a lane.

$\frac{107}{158}$ Washing The Stairs

Everyone washed the stairs like, you lived, there was six tenants up the hall, and every neighbour would wash their flight, one, and down to the next woman underneath them, and that woman underneath would come out, and she'd wash down to the next one,, everyone took their turn to wash down the stairs and all.

Bronze Plaque installed on Ross Road. Story no. 107/158. See no. 14 on page 8 and 9. Photo by Chris Reid.

There was six tenants up the hall and every neighbour would wash their flight down to the next woman underneath them and that woman would come out and wash the steps to the next one and so on. Everyone took their turn to wash the stairs and all.

1970s

108/158 Local Choir

The seagulls was the best choir on the road. They'd be on the Iveagh Baths wall, right outside our back window early morning. They'd drive you mad, listening to them – WA! WA! WA! We used to call that the Ross Road choir. The bins attracted them and whatever scraps of food they could get from them.

Someone used to snare the seagull and let it fly around the house. Another fella's Da would give the gull citric acid on bread then see if it would fly off or blow up. The acid in their stomach would react to the citric.

109/158 Toss School in The Yard

It was a great old road it was and there was great people around the road then. We used to be out the back there and play football and there used to be a wall out there at the back of us. There used to be a wall at the back of the yard there and they shaped out the goal posts, do you know what I mean, and we used to play football and all in the yard. And there used to be top toss there at the back. Where the Iveagh used to back onto the backyard and they used to do the gambling and that is years ago, even before I moved down. We used to be able to see them from my Auntie's window and I used to stand out with my uncle and see them. You are talking big money.

Some lost money and some won money as well – it was thousands. In the 1970s. Yeah two coins and there used to be blokes in there that used to flip tails and there used to be other lads who would flip heads. That is the way it worked do you know what I mean. Some bloke would go in and he would chance it and he would say a grand in the middle and it would start off from there. On the ground. Side bets as well and if he turned heads that would be two grand and you would have to get three and then throw them again and he gets heads again, and you get a few grand out of it. Into his hand and the two men in the middle get a nice few bob and throw it into their pocket and that is the way it works. You have to get three points or three hits, you know what I mean, and it all depends on how much is in the middle. Up to a hundred might watch.

Bronze Plaque installed on Ross Road. Story no. 105 & 109/158. See no. 13 on page 8 and 9. Photo by Chris Reid.

There was a toss school of a Sunday. Men would gather behind the Iveagh Baths which was our back yard. They'd have notes and coins in a pot on the ground in the middle of them. Side bets were taken as well. If you seen the cops coming you ran over shouting, 'Cops! Cops!', and the men all ran off. Occasionally I'd do that just to get the few bob left on the ground. The cops would be coming up the yard and they'd ask, 'What are you doing?' 'I'm hanging out the washing', I'd say and shake out the tea towel I kept over my shoulder.

Roebuck House, Clonskea, Dublin 14, Ireland. Phone 694225

27th Oct 76

Dear Bridie,

I got your letter yesterday – just as I had been thinking of you. Your letter seems to have taken a long time as it's dated for the 19th & the postmark is 18th which means it took a whole week. I have just got the list of prisoners – you are a great girl – so constant on the job!

Indeed I do remember the Fancy Dress Ball in the Union! I think there may only have been a couple of combs with paper over them! but I daresay you are right about the mouth organs & fiddle the Kerry girls had a fiddle I think – I remember Annie O'Farrelly as Robert Emmet. I also remember the job she had to get the Flour out of her hair – she had 'powdered' her hair in the style of his period & she looked splendid!

The North is a terrible business – I suppose it has to finish sometime, but when & how! It just goes on and on getting worse if anything – the whole country is in a mess & getting worse.
Anyway good luck to you & best wishes from Ireland – I don't suppose I'd know you now & I met you – it's so long since I saw you. All the best –

Cilla B.

Letter from Catalina McBride to Bridie Halpin, 1976. Image courtesy of Christopher Halpin and The Kilmainham Gaol Museum.

Letters From America

She used to correspond with Catalina McBride, Sean McBride's wife, and she used to get the lists of the prisoners, the people who were, not the prisoners but the people who they threw in prison, it didn't matter what or who they were, what the hell was the name of it? Internment. Bridie got a list from Catalina McBride and she was sending money over there and I remember her showing me a letter from the United States Government and the Irish Government and the English Government about what she was doing, she wasn't supposed to be sending money to this organisation. She was sending money anyway. Whether she was gathering funds or not but she was sending her own money, that I know. That would have been the early 1970s.

Relationships and The Flats

"When I got married I got a flat beside my Ma and Da's flat. My front room was next to my Da's front bedroom. When I had my fire lighting you could go into my Da's flat and into the front bedroom and put your hand on the wall. It would be roasting. I used to say to my Da that he owed me money for keeping his flat warm." [12]

When I first got married, I lived in a flat beside me Ma and Da's flat. Mine was only a one bedroom, me Ma had the two bedroom, but my front room was next door to my Da's front bedroom, and when I'd have my fire lighting, if you went up to my father's flat, and put your hand at his wall, it was roasting. I used to say to me Da he used to owe me money, because I used to keep his flat warm. Or if they wanted me, my Ma used to get the sweeping brush, and hit it off the skirtings, and I'd hear the knock in my flat and I knew Ma wanted me for something, and I'd look out my window, and my Ma would be looking out her window, if she wanted me for something.

12. See page 231

Before I lived in that flat, there used to be a woman, and her name was Mrs. Fitzgerald, and as a teenager, growing up, when I'd be in my bedroom, I used to hear Mrs. Fitzgerald in her bedroom, I'd hear the woman's kettle, getting put on, and I'd hear the kettle boiling, and I'd be lying in bed, and I'd used to say, 'Oh God Mrs. Fitzgerald, will you knock that kettle off, it will come through the wall at me.' When I got married, me husband was down the Corporation looking for a flat, and he rang me at work to say 'We're after getting a flat' and I says, 'Where?'. He tells me the address and I know it's Mrs. Fitzgerald's. 'I'm not taking that flat,' I said, 'because that's right next door,' I says to him, 'Go into that room, and go into the bedroom, and I bet you anything there's a plug there to plug something in' and it was. I knew what was going to be in the place before I moved in.

I could be up late looking at a picture, at two o'clock, and me Da always made sure that you'd rake the fire, you know, never leave a fire high, always rake it down low before you go to bed, but then when I'd go up to me Da the next day, me Da would say to me, you were up to three o'clock last night, and I'd say, 'How do you know?' 'I heard you raking the fire.' So there was sometimes you couldn't do things, because they'd hear you, do you know that type of thing, but, it was good like, and they was lovely people, and they were nice and warm, and the neighbours like Mrs. Forte next door to us. The landings were bigger then and during the summer when the weather was lovely my Ma and Mrs. Forte would bring two chairs out to the landing. They would open up the lobby windows, sit down and do knitting.

112/158 Fuel Donors

My brother had an old van. It had different coloured doors and things on it. He used to move things for people. For a time in the 1970s petrol was hard to come by. It was very expensive and you had to queue hours to get it. One day someone called the police onto the road about something else. They parked and went looking for someone or something. My Da happened to be looking out the window of his flat to see this fella – the brother – using a rubber hose to siphon petrol from the police vehicle into his van. Da says, 'Would you not go down and tell him I'm watchin' and when he comes up here I'll give it to him.' So I go down, walk across the road and whisper to him, 'You're bein' watched.' He says, 'The effing cops are up the road, will you leave me alone!' I says, 'No, It's me Da is watchin' you.' 'Fuck off!' He finishes a few moments later and drives off.

Pubs – Places to Meet

If you were looking for a fella for something and you didn't go to where he lived, you went to where he drank. And if you were enquiring and you needed this fella to do something you'd ask, 'Do you know where he drinks?' You wouldn't ask where does he live. Well some people got paid in pubs, you know, and that is where they went you know. I ended up drinking in the same pub me father drank in and today me son drinks there. I haven't been in a pub now for years. But even coming to the end of my drinking, the atmosphere was almost completely gone, you know. The main thing in the small local Dublin pubs was the camaraderie, people helping each other out, the singsong, and the sense of humour. I knew one man and he had no understanding of the value of money, so we were in a conversation discussing the price of a house. And someone said 50,000 pound that would cost like, and he said to me how many pints would you get for that. And when you told him how many pints you got for that then he could understand how much it was, which was true you know.

Many of the pubs around here are gone, such as O'Byrnes, O'Connell's – the Napper Tandy, Corbetts, Graces, Phelans. There are very few what I would call comfortable homely pubs left. There are some around Meath Street and that but nowadays you have to go out for a smoke so now I don't go into the pubs anymore but I still see them, you know, and they would say, 'Are you coming out for a pint later, Leo?' and I would say, 'No. You wouldn't buy me one when I was drinking.' But it's my family goes back to that area and say High Street in particular.

Men drinking in a pub in the 1970s. Photo courtesy of Eddie Hatton.

I ended up drinking in the same pub me Father drank in and today me son drinks there. The main thing in the small pubs was the camaraderie - the sing-song, the sense of humour. If you were looking for a fella to do something you wouldn't go to his house, you'd go to a pub. You'd ask where he drinks not where he lives. Many of the pubs around here are gone, such as O'Byrnes, O'Connells, Napper Tandy, Corbetts, Graces, Phelans . . .

.... 1970s

Paying Respects to Dev

114/158

The Castle was a great place to play as a kid. What are now the Castle Gardens used to be a football pitch. You would have to climb over the wall to play in there or go through a bunch of gaps between prefab buildings to get to it unless you could go through the building itself, which we weren't allowed to do. On the other side of the prefabs there was a handball court that was well used. I knew every nook and cranny of it.

When de Valera kicked the bucket I got a few days off school. When he was laying in state in the Castle the line to see him went all around the Castle yard out the gate and down the street. I wanted to pay my respects to the man for getting me off school. I knew a shortcut that led right up to near the front of the line. There was always a Garda on duty just inside the gate on Ship Street in a small hut. When it was slow they would play cards with you inside the hut to pass the time. Behind the hut was what we called the dungeon area. A walkway with low ceilings, very narrow with cell doors on either side. Damp and dark with a few light bulbs strung together. On the other side of the dungeon a little bit down there was some steps that led you up to the main Castle courtyard, this is where I would nip into the line. The Castle main building entrance wasn't too far from that. Inside the door was the condolence book and then inside one of the main rooms was Dev all laid out. It was an open coffin so you could see his face. My granny had died earlier that year and she was the first dead person I ever saw so I felt like an old hand at the death thing. In my mind as a nine year-old it was just some dead fella and no school. I'd nip into the line, sign the book inside the door, pay my respects, out the door, run around through the dungeon area again and back into the line for the same again. Jaysus, must have signed that book a dozen times.

About ten years later I was outside the main gate when Ronald Reagan was visiting. When his limo left the back window was down about three inches and he was sticking his hand out waving at the people. At least everybody thought it was his hand so I got to see Ronnie's hand at the Castle too.

Bronze plaque installed on Bride Street. Stories no. 113 & 145/158. See no. 21 on page 8 and 9.
Photo by Chris Reid.

I never really had a conversation with my father. Sometime in the 1960's he caught me mitching from school and gave me an awful hiding. Ripped the clothes off me, lashed me with the belt and punched me in the eyes.

115/158 Lost Brother

My brother died but he got cremated, I was able to go over that time I got him cremated and I brought him back and he's in Mount Jerome. He's in with the mother and sure she was always worried about him. He was away for over 20 years, disappeared. He just disappeared for 20 years.

But my granny was looking for him all that time. Didn't my granny go to England, didn't she try and trace him with Interpol and all. We couldn't trace him. They couldn't find him so he didn't want to be found. We tried. He might have been locked up! Ah no, if he was we'd have known. Just didn't want to be found.

Didn't hear from him for over 20 years, just appeared one day! He was missing for more than 20 years, then he suddenly appeared. Now he's dead and buried, that's the man I got cremated. We never questioned him, he never opened his mouth where he was or what he did, we just didn't know. Never asked him any questions whatsoever. If he wanted to tell us he could have told us but he didn't want to do that so we didn't ask. So then he died and I got him cremated and brought the ashes back with me and put him in with the mother.

116/158 Hard

The front room was small. A big table in the middle and a glass case and the old record player and the flowers in the window and curtains. The records – Dean Martin, Sammy Davis Junior and all that and Englebert. My father, he was more Frank Sinatra and all that, you know what I mean, and into singing in pubs and all of that and going to the Transport Club in Camden Street and the good times. He used to sing all over there. And Paddy Comber or Frank Sinatra he would sing you know. He used to sing in the Transport Club. I was really young and I never really had a conversation with my father and my father was really rough and all he was. When I was mitching from school he would give me an awful hiding. Smack me with his belt in the face and push my eyes out and all, crazy you know what I mean – he was on the gargle yeah. Like very hard – do you know what I mean? And I used to be terrified. Like rip the clothes off me and lash me with the belt just for mitching from school. I mean I did nothing really.

Bronze Plaque installed on the Ross Road. Story no. 116/158. See no. 16 on page 8 and 9. Photo by Chris Reid.

1970s

$\frac{117}{158}$ The Lounge Boy

I was fifteen or sixteen when I worked at the Man of Aran pub on Aran Quay. It was one of the really posh places to go and have something to eat. At one stage it was nice but I always remember the owner was very, very mean. I worked there with my friend Robert, we each got one pound a night for working there. Then a friend, whose name I can't remember, he was nineteen or twenty and was the chief barman in the Napper Tandy pub on Bride Street. They were short staffed for lounge boys and he rang us up and said we could come over and work. Our wages increased from one pound to three pound a night. The owner Mrs. McHugh a very nice person, and if we worked the full three nights she would make it a tenner. It was always night time work because we would have been in school.

It was dark. An old style bar – the bar and the wall were close together, you went in the front door, the bar was on the left side. The bar ran away from you, the toilet was at the far end. There was a curve at the end then right through to the lounge. You went into the lounge and downstairs into a kind of bigger room in the back left-hand side. There was a bit of a bar and this was the serving area that was about half way down at the back. A nice atmosphere for the people there.

This would've been '75, '76 around that time. Tough working men used the bar. They were forceful, talking loudly, a swagger. A sort of confidence. Some were skinheads wearing bomber jackets and denim jackets, which I did myself. Having being used to the Man of Aran, which was very reserved, this was very different. If someone said 'Boo!' to someone else that could easily start a fight. There was a walk between the bar and the lounge bar area and a door between the two of them. We heard something going on in the lounge. The two of us went in together – I walked in, Robert behind me, and I remember a full pint coming straight at me – the lager still in the glass – I ducked and it hit Robert in the chest the glass smashed on the ground. A row was taking place. They were throwing glasses and bottles at each other. We were outsiders yet we were insiders in this place. Most times the hard chaws would be nice to us because we were serving them beer. I don't remember them ever fighting us – just with each other.

It was the local tough pub. There were other pubs, The Castle and The Lord Edward, which were quieter. Passers-by wouldn't come in to the Napper Tandy as it was a 'regulars only' type pub, a bit of a closed shop. The only reason I was there was because I was working there. They were very generous to us, used to get good tips from them.

Some people from the Model Lodging House drank there. There was an older man. The other barman was tall, handsome and that, you'd think he was from Spain. I remember this older man eyeing the other barman every time he passed. The barman, he was probably working full-time there he would say, 'Mind your man there.' He probably pointed him out to us. Another man was called Michael. He was in his sixties. They used to say that Michael was the woman because everyone would be riding Michael. He was very camp and affected but poor. He wasn't dressed up or anything. He'd wear a trench coat. He would come in for his drink and sit down. The other barman would have said, 'You see him? He's gay.' I had never seen anyone who was gay.

There was a little lane to the side to the left side of the pub. There was an entrance door in the back way, that led out to the lane. It also led upstairs. One night we were finishing up – counting the money and all that with this other chap. There was banging – suddenly someone kicked the back door in – fellas with balaclavas came in. I was chased through the bar and back out. They had weapons, I was running – the fear – being chased around. I can never remember a conclusion to the raid. I found a place to hide. I was scared – people with weapons looking for money and I might've known where it was. I may have left at that time when the place was raided. I don't even know if I told me mother.

Bride Street and Werburgh Street in the 1980s. The Napper Tandy pub can be seen on the right.
Photo by Sean Redmond, courtesy of Fergus Redmond.

118/158 Showbusiness Dreams

I used to love your man Brendan Grace. Now I didn't know him personally but I met him a few times. He's around the same age as I am. I'm nearly fifty-five. I'd say Brendan is about the same age but I used to do things when I was a young man that he is making money out of now. I used to act the mick like Frank Spencer, you know Michael Crawford*. I'd have fellas falling on the floor spilling their drink. 'What you doing working in the Corporation you should be on the stage.' I never really followed it up. Maybe I might get a bolt of lightning some day. I'm gonna do it now and go for it.

If I sing a Nat King Cole song, I do it as close to his voice, particularly if I have music behind me. The scene is set up properly. In a room with good amplification. I actually feel him inside me when I'm singing. A fella said, 'Janey Mack I don't know how you do that. I mean you're Dublin born and you're singing a coloured man's song. It's totally unbelievable.' Who knows maybe some day I'll get the chance. Thinking back now I heard Charlie Landsborough interviewed. It took him twenty-five years to get on the road. Charlie Landsborough I'm talking about. Twenty-five years because he, like myself, he worked in various different jobs. We call it 'housing attendants', they have different names over in England. Me Mam used to say I could have done it professionally a long time ago but I didn't have the push in me, d'ye know what I mean. You have to have the push.

119/158 Joining The British Army

You couldn't do that in Dublin in the 70s. I know people who did it before that but when the troubles kicked off there was people going around the flats saying, you know, you have to knock it on the head. What do you call it, like republicans, which is understandable and the feeling was high at the time, considering that the government tried to smuggle guns up to them. There was...and anyone that I knew who wanted to join the army and was older than me, would have joined the BA (British Army) in the 60s. But I know for a fact that there was people in the BA who lived in areas close to me who left as soon as the Troubles kicked off up the north. I don't know if they left of their own feelings, or because of the knock on the door, but they left anyway.

---

* The actor who played Frank Spencer in Some Mothers Do Have 'Em

Marriage – An Escape

My two sisters and my elder brother, and John my younger brother, all married within a few years, they were all married nearly before they were twenty or twenty-one, so that left meself and me father and Henry the youngest brother for a few years, living there, and then I got married, Henry got married, the two of us got married, so probably within, if my mother died when I was thirteen, about 1968, by 1978 or 1980, within twelve years, the six of us had married, the six children, within twelve years, and me father was left there on his own. So I think marriage was a bit of an escape, you know, and we married young. And each of us bought a house, which was probably a bit unusual at the time, each of us saved up. But my three brothers, I worked in a pub in Francis Street as a barman, and I got them all jobs as lounge boys, and they worked the Friday night, the Saturday night, and the Sunday night, and they got three pound a night, so you got paid on Sunday, so each of them had day jobs, you know, and then they worked the three nights of the weekend.

My Grandmother

My grandmother was a very well known dealer, in the place called the Daisy Market and that was over beside the fruit market. There was a thing in the paper about it when she died because she was so well known in the Liberties. Her name was Kate, Kate McGee. And I used to bring the pram over to the market for her on Saturday morning and be on the stall with her, and she would be in the pub. It's over near the fruit market, actually I think that the pub is gone now. The fruit market is Smithfield is off Capel Street. You could head down to Smithfield from there but the Dublin fruit market it's still there and the main entrance is the same type of brickwork as Nicholas Street and it goes back to the same time. And the entrance to the Daisy Market is still there but it's not open any more. And they sold curtains and second hand shoes and clothes and all that type of stuff.

The Daisy Market, it's between Capel Street and Church Street and it would bring you down to the Law Library there. My cousins, which are her granddaughters, still sell in markets around Meath Street and that. They are carrying on the tradition. Things are just handed down

The Liberties loses 'good-looking Kate'

The ancient Liberties has lost yet another pillar with the death, at 83, of Mrs. Catherine Magee, "good-looking Kate." A hawker of secondhand clothes in the area for decades, Kate leaves behind a social, cultural and economic gap, one which the Liberties people feel to the heart.

Amongst her claims to fame were that she started the first travelling clothes shop in Ireland, that she was cured of an incurable disease at the grotto in St. Catherine's of Meath St., and—a shrewd business woman—once sold a "lost" coffin at a handsome profit to a firm in Cook St.

Born in Sth. Earl St. in 1888, Kate married a boot-and-shoe maker, and reared nine children on the proceeds of her stall in Francis St. Her husband died 35 years ago.

MODEL-T FORD

With a family to raise, aKte took to the Provinces — by horse and cart to the Broadstone, from there by rail to Dundalk, Athy, Loughrea or Ballinasloe. With the changing times, she laid her hands on a Model-T Ford and was driven by her eldest son Con to her destinations, a practice she kept up until 15 years ago.

In the country they still speak of her, and another son, John, who maintains the "business" has been deluged with questions on her welfare in "the four corners of Ireland".

Her "coffin" exploit is still retold in the gossip snugs of the Liberties — snugs where Kate's wit was razor sharp after a day's toil. She bought the celebrated coffin at a lost-property auction in Amiens Street Station, and traded it to a firm in Cook Street, then the home of casket-makers.

Her cure at the Lourdes grotto in Meath Street was never officially recognised — but that didn't stop her from making two thanksgiving trips in the 1950s . . . to the original shrine in France.

Kate was ill for several weeks before her death, but was as attentive and merry as on her wedding day.

Kate clothed generations, regiments of Dubliners and they did her justice at the funeral. When she met people who looked alike, she used to remark: "The name of the Maker is on the blade." In "good-looking Kate" the Maker cut a gem, or as they say in the Liberties, He stayed up all night on the mould.

— Liam O Cuanaigh

Troops paid extra for 'tough' tests

British troops are being paid extra money to become "guinea pigs" to find out how tough the army can get in the North.

Top secret training is being carried out at the British Government's chemical defence establishment at Porton Down in Wiltshire. Part of the training mock Derry-style riots and in these servicemen act the part of IRA men.

The volunteers can be bombarded with riot-control gas and other weapons while they also test protective clothing which the army may use in the future.

A team of doctors will be on hand during the tests. The men who part in the two-week experiment will get up to £10 a week extra pay.

Several readers from Dublin and other parts of the country have written to me about immunisation against diphtheria, whooping cough and tetanus. Since these illnesses are of major importance and carry serious consequences, that include death for some patients, I propose to devote my column this evening to the subject.

Immunisation is a prophylactic measure which aims at protecting children against diphtheria, whooping cough and tetanus. Public Health Authorities and doctors have done an enormous amount of work in promoting immunisation. So good indeed are the results of their efforts that one seldom hears about a case of diphtheria nowadays. Unfortunately the very success of their work is tending to create complacency among many parents and this is where a word of warning must be given.

Some children have been immunised but failure to complete the course of injec-

1970s

I remember it was often freezing cold. It was just like a lane with a gate at either end. It had a roof on it and stalls down each end of it and they were full of tables with clothes and curtains and anything that you could sell. It was open both ends and it was bloody freezing you know. So, Dublin dealers are unbelievable with their generosity. I have seen it first hand you know and a lot of them lent money to people. And like I used to see people coming to my grandmother and she wouldn't be going chasing her for it. Then I have seen people coming into the market where my grandmother was, and she was a fine big woman, and she never spoke of anything like that. I never heard her bad mouthing anyone – the same with my grandmother on my mother's side. She was from off Abbey Street there, from the tenements in Abbey Street. And completely different from my other grandmother, but totally the same generosity. You know they didn't see any bad in people. If someone had something wrong with them they would just say, 'God help them,' you know. Yeah she died my grandmother the dealer in 1972 and there was only six months between her and my father. It was one of the biggest funerals I have ever seen around there. They put a thing in the paper about her saying that she was a well-known pillar of the community in the Liberties. I remember my father showing it to me and he was so proud you know. But very decent people. I am going to dig it out.

Opposite Page: Evening Press, 29 July 1972. Image courtesy of Leo Magee.
Below: The Daisy Market, 2009. Photo by Chris Reid.

Boys' School

The school I went to was St. Audoen's, it was tough, it was a tough part of town. Huge classes, The Principal brought out a book there recently about St. Audoen's. I saw a photograph recently, I think there was thirty-six or something, thirty-eight in the class. How on earth they coped with it? There was a lot of beatings too. I was on the Board of Management then in later years, the first of the Boards of Management when they came in, I would have been mid-twenties at the time, and they asked me to go on it, and I remember going in, and into classes, and smelling the unwashed bodies, because people didn't wash, you could tell young lads that pissed themselves in bed and all – thirty or forty young bodies. Well there were no bathrooms of course. I mean out of the thirty or forty fellows that was in the class, there wasn't a bathroom between anybody I suppose, when you think of it.

Mrs. Slyman

The chap that lives underneath me, his mother, Mrs. Slyman she lived across the road, facing me, that woman was a beautiful woman too, they were all lovely neighbours, but that woman sticks out in me head too, because that woman, I think she was from the country and, Jesus, she had a load of them, there was about ten of them. She was in, facing, No. 11, that's the last hall, C, D, 11D she would have been in. She was a lovely woman, Jesus she was a lovely woman, and she did all her own baking, she baked all her own bread, she baked all her own things, she baked everything, but she was a very hardworking woman, she used to work over in Harcourt Street Hospital for the Children. And they'd all be out in school, because I used to play with her daughter, and I used be in her house, and she used to make all their dinners, and put them all in the ovens, and when they'd come home. If you got up during the night, like where I lived on the Ross Road, I was looking over into somebody else's hall, because that's the way it was, you know what I mean, you're looking into someone else's home, and they're looking into yours, so if I got up during the night, as a kid like, and come three o'clock, four o'clock, five o'clock – Mrs. Slyman's light was always on, where she'd be washing her floors, before she'd go to bed, she'd be after probably washing all the delft and doing more cooking, making apple cakes and things like that, now for her family she kind of did it, but she was always on the go, she was always a real healthy type of woman, always doing things. Yea, she was a country woman, but a lovely woman, she was.

.... 1970s

Annie Slyman – mother of the Slyman kids. Photo and caption courtesy of Margaret Slyman.

19

The yards behind the flats on Bride Street. Francis Moore is on the left and Philip Forte is on the right.

80s

Photo courtesy of the Freer family.

The Visit

124/158

One year back in the early 80s, probably '80 or '81 my mother was sick in hospital and I went over to see her and my aunt Bridie happened to be on vacation at that time. And we went up to see her, she was in, I forget the name of the hospital but it was actually the North Dublin Union before it was a hospital. And I saw her walking around looking at the windows and I didn't know what she was doing. But later when she died, I found all this stuff, this is where she had been incarcerated, and she was walking around there like she knew the place, you know, the windows and…it was unbelievable. When I thought back about it later, you know. She had been transferred, most of the people who were on hunger strike out of Kilmainham in the 1920s were moved over to North Dublin Union. She never spoke about it – no not a word. I think if there had been such a defining moment in your life really that changed her I'm sure, it changed the course of her life for sure, that she wouldn't have said to me, her nephew, Christy, 'I don't know if you knew this but I stayed here during the Civil War you know.' It's unbelievable, that takes a lot to be able to keep your mouth shut for something like that, it's so emotional a thing, it's incredible. That's when the whole Long Kesh H Block hunger strike thing was going on, you think that must have just brought her back to all that as well.

1980s

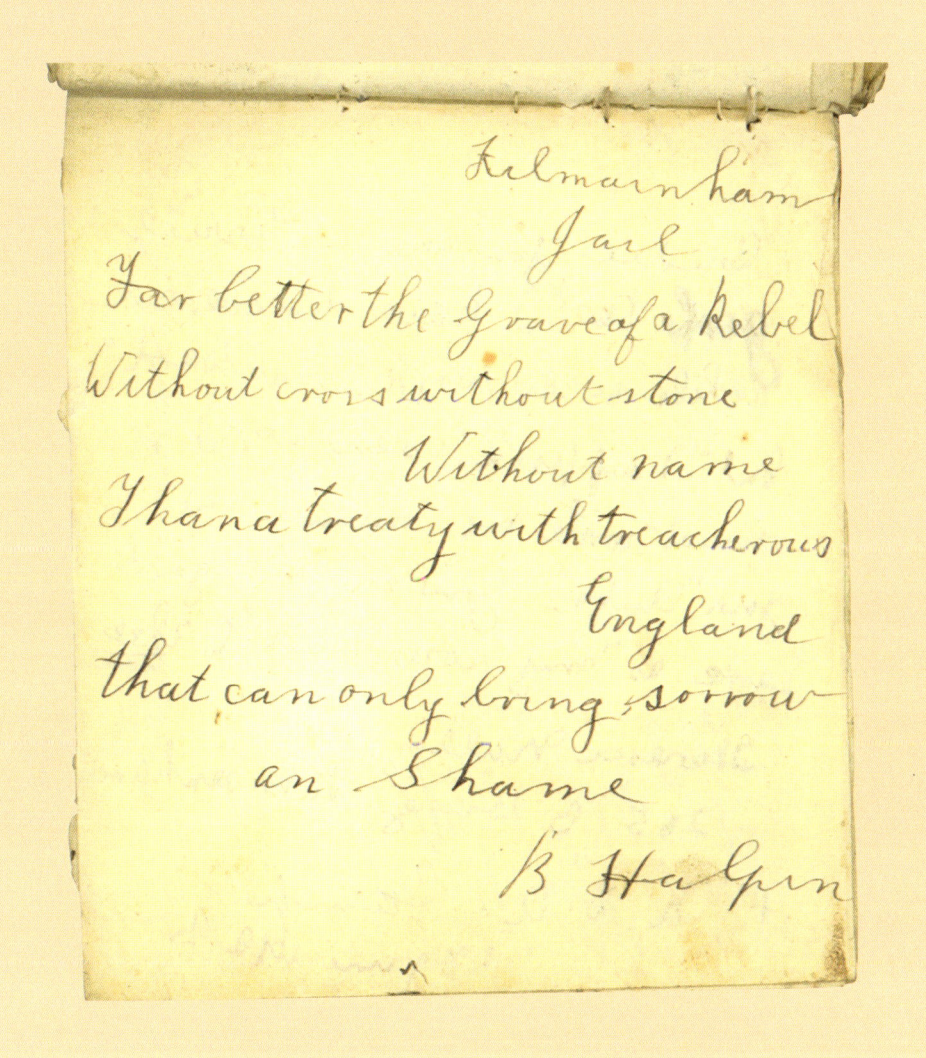

> Kilmainham Jail
>
> Far better the Grave of a Rebel
> Without cross without stone
> Without name
> Than a treaty with treacherous England
> that can only bring sorrow an Shame
>
> B Halpin

A page from Bridie Halpin's jail journal. Image courtesy of Christopher Halpin and the Kilmainham Gaol Museum.

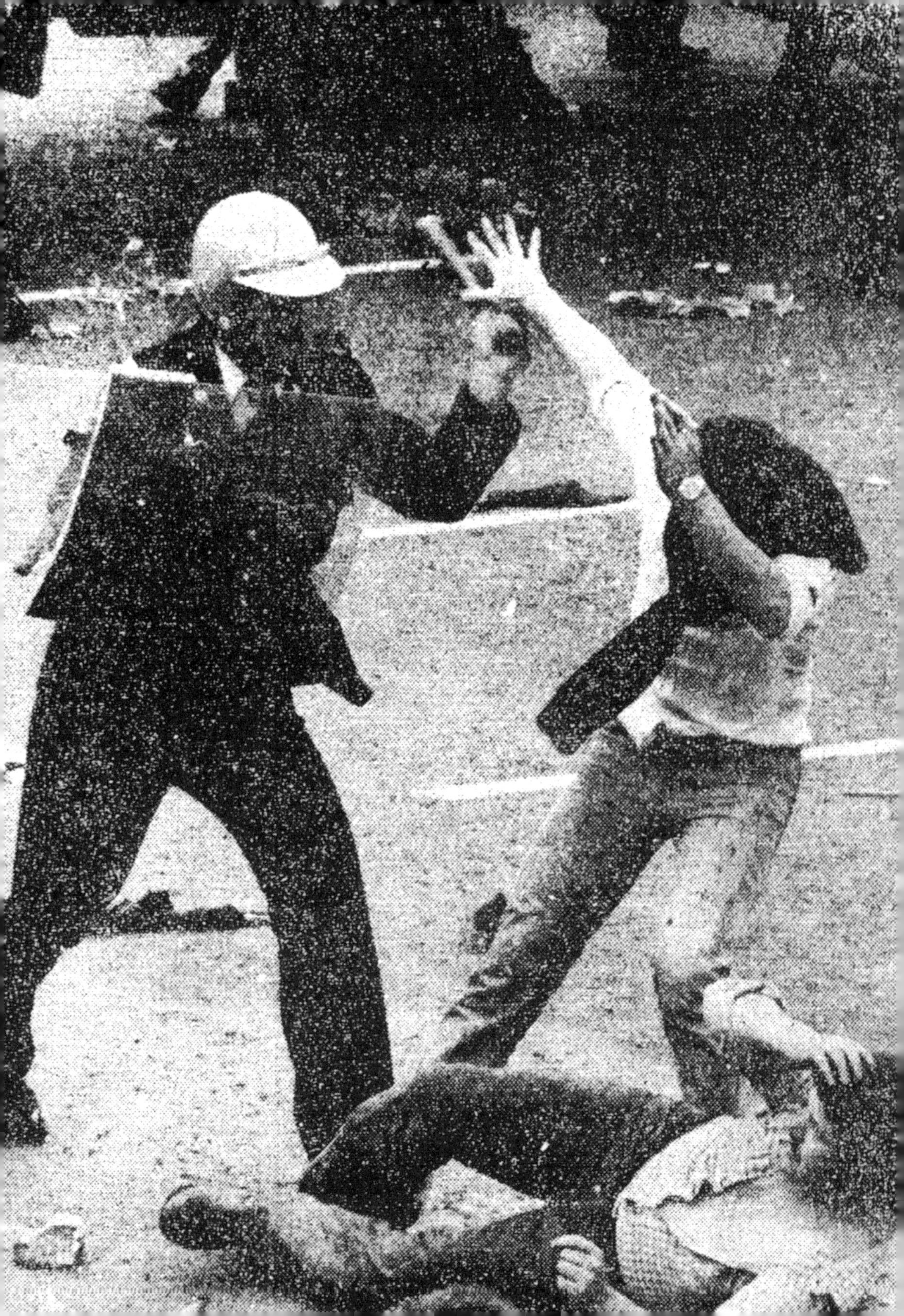

125/158 On Both Sides

I do remember the riot at the British Embassy down in Ballsbridge and I mean I was there myself then. Well the tension was very high, very, very high and that is what brought that about. We were all young, you know, and I don't know if that type of thing is in my blood. You see now, I didn't say to myself even though I was young, here is a chance for me to cause some trouble with the police and all that. Now I grew up in a rough area but I was never in trouble with the police. I was there because of the way that I felt inside – I was genuinely annoyed. You know, to me, well, what really pissed me off at the time was the Thatcher government, you know, and her attitude towards the Irish and just a sheer annoyance and upset. And you would have seen people there going, 'We are here to cause trouble. With the police' and 'We don't like the police.' I was there because of the way that I felt about the way that Irish people were being treated. And that government in particular ran her own people into the ground and if you look at the miners' strike and Scargill and all that. And that divided families for ever you know. But that to me was tyranny like and it was her in particular.

I got a few smacks. Yeah, I did get a few smacks and I mean you couldn't have helped it. I mean if you were fighting or not you just got caught up in it, you know. I was shouting, I didn't throw anything, that is not in me, even now, you know. I threw a couple of digs but I would never pick up a weapon – even now like. Was it raining? No, I don't think so. I can't remember the date, exactly. Those people who were with me I can't remember if they were wearing hoods over their heads because it was raining or hiding their faces, I can't remember. But there were certainly a lot wearing those parka jackets, you know, hoods up and all that. But the police were heavy handed. Hit me straight to the head. I was just intended on getting away and I didn't feel the pain 'til afterwards and I didn't feel the pain at the time and I knew that I had been hit.

I remember then in the 70s when I was in the army and there was some guys up on the roof in Mountjoy and we were called in as the riot squad. And I was standing there with my helmet and me visor and my shield and my baton, you know. And looking up at all my neighbours on the roof. Luckily nothing came to it, you know. I am glad that I didn't have to and I don't think I even would have. But I was like thinking this is crazy – they all know who I am up there. They will break me Mam's windows. That time I was on the opposite side, but I was there that day in Ballsbridge definitely because of the way that I felt and not because of trouble. Just to make the point, you know, and I would be there today still if the same thing happened, I would be there again you know.

Police and protesters on Merrion Row, 18 July, 1981. Irish Independent, Monday, July 20, 1981.

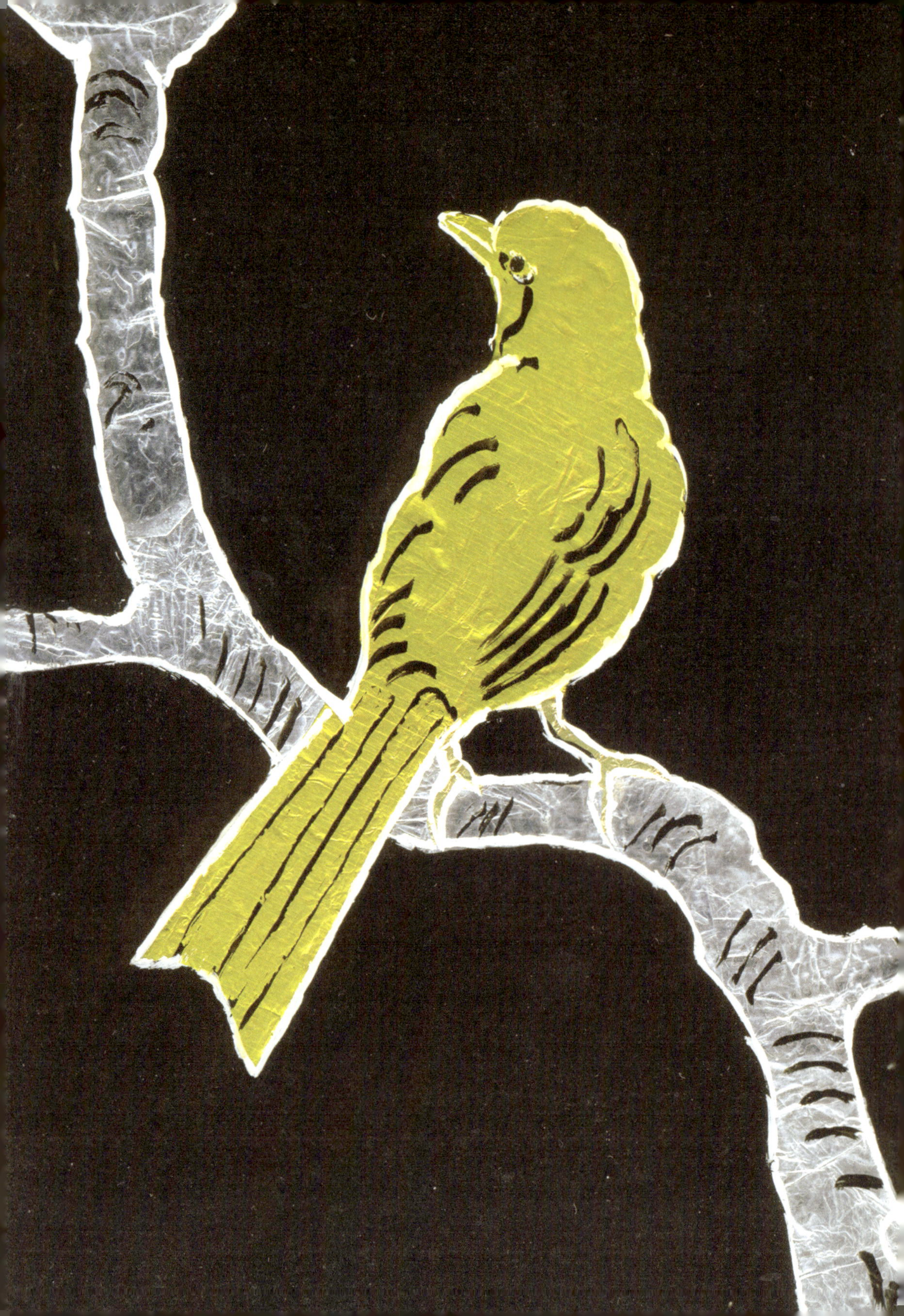

126/158 Dabbling

I wasn't living in the area at the time but I was close by. I was living in Blackpitts. It was 1981, yea, 1981 and I travelled around for eight months with some friends in Europe, came back to Dublin, it was when I came back to Dublin, after being away, the first time, that they were dabbling, nibbling, the guys. I was dabbling with them, a couple of skin-pops. Didn't know anything about how to cook it up or anything, they were the ones that were dabbling, so I was with them a few times. For about six months, at that stage, I stayed in Dublin, and once or twice I might have used, that was about it, wasn't really my thing I thought. Left, went to London for a year to work, came back to Dublin and they were all doing it, and I was hanging around with them and they were all stoned, and I wasn't, and that would be like nearly every night, well initially it was just at weekends and stuff but I'd hang round with them, all the time I was just hanging out with them, and they were stoned. Anyway, when I came back from being away travelling, and the guys were all dabbling, and as I say, I sampled and tested the thing. When I eventually left, after going to London for a year, coming back to Dublin, in my early twenties I went back to Britain – well, Edinburgh. I was twenty-three, I think I got it when I was twenty-three.

127/158 Gas Explosion

Around 1984/85 there was a big gas explosion in Nicholas Street and I don't know if you heard about that. But there was a big build up of gas, underneath those red brick buildings along Nicholas where you come off Christchurch. And the gas company was working around there and the mother and the daughter were blown out through the door, there was no one killed luckily enough. So there is gas there now and they had to put us up in the hotel for a few days. They put us up in the one that Bono owns now. I still have the towels. The Clarence Hotel.

'I use foil used to wrap sweets and Easter eggs. Joseph Slyman taught me the technique when I used to live on the Ross Road forty years ago.' Caption and picture by Fran O'Connor (085 715 2773).

1980s

Nicholas Street 1980s – prior to road widening. The entrance to McDonald's pub can be seen in the background. Photo courtesy of Daniel Lyons.

McDonald's Pub, Patrick's Street, 1980. This pub along with the car park were demolished to make way for blocks of apartments in the 1990s. Copyright: Dublin City Public Libraries.

128/158 Petty Crime

There was always petty crime. There was some peer pressure – not enough for me to get into it yet too much for me to just say no and move on. Some of the heads progressed to more involved crime. Drugs started coming in, I would say late 70s early 80s. Some of the more 'progressive' petty criminals who were older than me started doing the gear and it went from there. Handbag snatching was the main income for these fellas. They wouldn't do it locally though as everyone knew them, they'd go into town to do it, Grafton Street area mainly. With that said a few years further down the line they would do it locally as they were too far gone to care. For the girls it was the shoplifting. Late 70s and 80s had a lot of drug use – bad times, sad times...

I think drugs had an effect on everyone that lived there. It hit hard with my generation but I wouldn't call it a disaster though. You have to look at the big picture with the area as a whole. The age group affected – not every block had kids of that age. The total number of people in a block as compared to the number doing the gear. So if you work out the numbers, flats times average number of people per flat as compared to the actual junkies then the percentage would be small, although they would have a major effect on all around them. I think a lot people of my age group in the flats didn't see much of a future. The Irish economy at the time was awful although I don't think they would have known the meaning of that comment. Ill education at its best. Sort of a 'nothing to lose' thing.

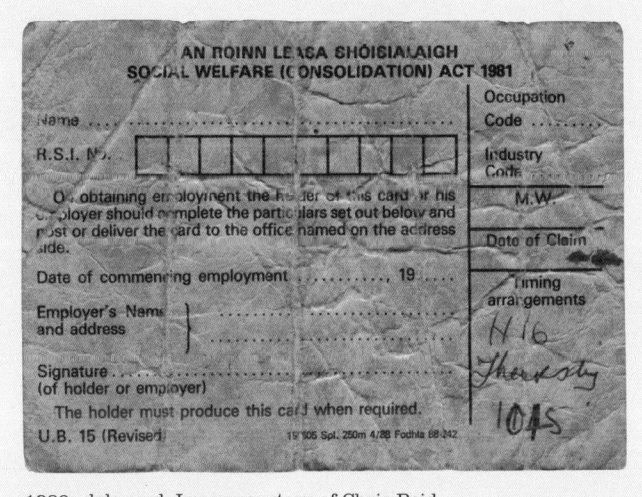

1980s dole card. Image courtesy of Chris Reid.

During the 1980's there was still no hot water in the flats. I had to go round to the Iveagh for a bath. I'd pay a few pence and go upstairs. There were separate rooms where you had your bath. I'd go mostly of a Saturday. By times I'd meet people who were in the same predicament as myself.

Iveagh Baths

129/158

I was born in High Street and when I got married first for a few years I lived in Nicholas Street. I like living in the Liberties, it's the same all over, the same type of people. The early 1980s I was living there and recently all of those places have been renovated and they are more like luxury apartments. Until that time at the early 1980s you still had to go to Iveagh Baths years ago for a bath. You would pay a few pence and you would go upstairs into cubicles. They were the swimming baths and they used to have all separate rooms upstairs, and you would have a bath there. You couldn't do it every day because of work and that, you would go for a bath on a Saturday morning and you would meet people who were in the same predicament as yourself.

Above: The Iveagh Baths, 1980. Photo courtesy of Irish Architectural Archive. Left: Bronze Plaque installed on Bride Road. Story no. 129/158. See no. 9 on page 8 and 9. Photo by Chris Reid.

1980s ....

130/158 New Parking Meters

In the early 80s a lot of the lads would make money by minding the cars. Fellas would park on Bride Street and the Rosser to collect the dole from Werburgh Street. 'Watch your car mister' and the fella might give ye five pence or ten pence or fifty pence if you were really lucky, or nothing at all. I was never a big fan of minding the cars and didn't do it often – too much self respect I think. I probably would have been about fifteen or sixteen, it was the early 1980s. Some of the lads would do it all day every day and make a good few bob. Anyway in the mid 80s the parkin' fellas came in and put in parking meters. One of the neighbours wasn't too happy about that. Parking meters cutting into his profits and all. He'd be out there when it was really dark with his hacksaw cutting the meters off the poles. Then they'd be back the next week putting new ones in. He gave up after about six months. Always brings a smile to my face when I think about it....

131/158 New Resident

I was offered a place in Ballymun and I wouldn't take it. And in 1986 they offered me Ross Road and I took it. Then when I got in there was kids breaking my windows all the time and every time I would get the window fixed with the Corpo they would break them. They were just kids trying to break in for the fun of it and trying to rob. I got broken into eight or nine times and they were breaking in all the time no matter what. They get in the windows. The police at that time they were OK, but if you got the guards they would know then who did and then they would beat you up. And you don't get the guards involved, you had to do it another way. Now there was some very bad apples in Ross at the time, but there was good apples, but I met the bad apples trying to break into my window. They got a big surprise one day because then I got fed up and I had my windows blocked up. I put heavy wood on it, inside the whole lot. My windows were blocked up inside and no glass at all and I was very happy with that. Even the council sent me letters saying you want to get the windows fixed and I said I don't care about them blocked up and I don't care about fire, so long as I don't get robbed. The road was quite safe when I had my windows well blocked up and I was happy. There was also a lot of neighbours on the road who would keep an eye on the place anyway and there was good neighbours at the time. And I met good neighbours on the road and they got to know me over the years and they would just keep an eye on the place. They

Most of the buildings in this picture (1980s) of Bride Street, Werburgh Street and the entrance to Derby Square have been replaced by Jurys car park. Photo by Sean Redmond, courtesy of Fergus Redmond.

don't tell you but if they see what is going on they would let you know anyway. It stopped over the years then and they stopped breaking in. They might have moved out and then a lot of them were thrown out of the road, a lot of them died and passed away. My windows were blocked up for eleven years.

1980s

The Store Detective

I did it for seventeen years like. I worked in all the major shops and I was in Champion Sports for three years and I was awarded security guard of the year from all the branches. Some of the biggest shoplifters in the town would be in some shop that I would be working in and when they saw me, it would be, 'Sorry, I didn't know you were working here.' And they would walk back out and the manager used to be amazed by this. And he would say, 'Jesus you must be a tough fucker you.' 'No,' I'd say, 'I grew up with most of them and I'd drink with them now and again, you know.' I would tell them that straight off and that is why they wanted me there, you know. I had respect off them, many people who went into security work the wrong way, you know, I have seen them going home from work and getting jumped on, you know. I caught people robbing – don't get me wrong, but I would take the stuff off them, throw them out of the shop and bar them and they would never come again. But I have seen people in the same situation getting them charged, and all that. And that would create a lot of hostility between the people buying in the shops and the people working in the shops. I never had that problem in my life – never. I was able to mingle with them, you know, and lived day-to-day life with the people who were in town trying to rob the shops. But as I said they wouldn't come in when I was around because they had respect, you know, for people from the same background.

There was some desperate ones – people addicted to drugs, God help them, and then there was the professionals, you know, they'd wear the suit, carry the briefcase – rob to order. Robbers, they have more rights than the person trying to protect the shop and they know that. They make things easier for them in the last few years and we had a security system which worked with tags on the clothes and if you tried to pass out the door the alarm would set off. But they found a way around that. Without having to damage the clothes they got a big carrier bag and lined it with tin foil. Neutralise the alarm. They are always one step ahead. But great people, you know. I have often gone to see Dublin playing at Croke Park and I would be on my way back and I would be in pubs on the Northside. And there would be drinks sent over to me and that would be unheard of for a store detective. And the donor would say, 'Fair play to you – you didn't get me nicked and all.'

You know it's the worse job in the world, I did it for seventeen years – security work. I didn't realise how bad it was until I got out, you know.

.... 1980s

SECURITY OFFICERS REQUIRED

Security Officers required for city centre company.

Static/Patrol work.

Aged 30 to 45 years.

Excellent character references required.

Experienced men preferred.

Good wages and conditions.

Details of age, experience if any to BOX NPT 781

Job advertisement from a newspaper, late 1970s. Image courtesy of Chris Reid.

1980s

$\frac{133}{158}$ Mother and Daughter

I couldn't leave her alone to cook or anything, so I had to give up the sewing, the day work. I was here all day with my mother and then someone would come in and sit with her while I was at work at night. Her memory went. It was hard on me. I nursed her for seven years on my own and for me at that particular time it was from bed to work. It was a complete day so I couldn't leave her that long but I've no regrets. I did what I could and that was it. Well the situation for me was I contacted Friends of the Elderly. They weren't much help to me as they didn't work in the evenings. They were willing to help me during the day but I didn't need help during the day because I was here all day. You see the cleaning job was from five in the evening to nine at night and it was then I needed somebody but it wasn't their fault either. Their schedule didn't suit me.

She didn't forget my name but she used to mix me up if anyone came in they'd say, 'How is Margaret?' that's my name, and she'd say, 'Who's Margaret?' and they'd say 'That's your daughter,' and she'd say, 'I don't have a daughter, I only have a son.' Now the next day would be the reverse she wouldn't have a son she'd have a daughter and then she'd say to me, 'I gave you five pounds yesterday and I got no change.' That went on all the time and she'd keep that up until ever I'd give her a fiver. If I gave her a fiver now she wouldn't have a clue where she put it. It would come back to me anyway but this was going on all the time. 'I gave you five pounds yesterday and I got no change. I didn't bring you up that way. I brought you up properly to give change to the person who owns the money,' and I'd say, 'There's your fiver,' and that would end it. But she got into little situations like that. Well I got used to it. I'm not easily upset. I'm a placid type of person anyway.

Family Dispute

I had something to eat with me wife then I went out. I said to her if there's any phone calls for me tell them I'm gone down to the club. I was expecting a phone call from me brother Sean and I said I'm going down to the club for a game of snooker and I said if there are any phone calls you know where to find me. I don't believe I was down the club for an hour when I got a phone call. It was me brother, Eamonn. 'What's wrong with you?' He said 'You want to go home quick,' he says, 'Mam is after being taken into hospital.' So I said, 'Is she going to the hospital or on her way?' 'They're in the process of taking her to The Mater.' I said, 'OK I'll be down as soon as I can.' So I got into the Mater and the doctor was doing tests on her and Eamonn, Sean, Joseph and me two sisters, Eithne and Deirdre were sitting together and the doctor came out and he hadn't met me so Sean called me over and he introduced me. The doctor said, 'Anthony can I have a word with you? Would you mind stepping into the room here. I'm after speaking to the rest of the family and looking at you in comparison to the rest of the family they seem to be on edge. You

Interior of a flat on Bride Street. Photo courtesy of the Freer family.

seem to be a fairly calm person,' he said, 'can I tell you something?' I said, 'Yes Doctor, tell away.' 'To tell you the truth your mother is on a respirator. The machine is keeping your Mam alive. We need the machine urgently. I'm asking you can we turn the machine off.' I said, 'Why are you asking me? Me father is out there, me brothers, me sisters are out there why are you asking me?' He said, 'Because you seem to be a very calm person and a very understanding person.' 'Well,' I said, 'work away.' So I went out and extended my deepest sympathy that mammy had passed away, course me dad didn't know what to do and I ran over and gave him a big hug. 'Look Da she's gone to a better place. You don't want to see your wife on a machine for the rest of her life. That's not on.' So Da said, 'Let's go family.' Course me brother went for me. Eamonn went for me. He stuck me up against the wall. Eamonn's short. I'm five foot nine Eamonn is only five foot seven. 'What are you telling me Mam is dead for?' 'Look brother I don't want to fight with you, Mammy is gone to a better place, so don't fight with me.' I haven't spoke to him since. Mammy passed away in 1980.

135/158 Leaving Home

Any jobs that I applied for I used my brother's address in Templeogue as I wouldn't have a hope in hell of getting the job if I put down my real address. I learned that I had to look after myself, nobody else could do that for me. In Ireland at the time it felt like the employer was doing you a favour employing you. It shouldn't be like that. A job should be a partnership with a sort of win-win outlook for both you and the employer. In Ireland it was a 'Do what I tell you and shut-up.' I was never very good at the 'shut-up' part. Ireland was a mess and I wanted a better future than what I thought Ireland could offer. I left when I was twenty-two. Moving to the States was difficult but I always wanted to get away. When I stepped off the plane I didn't know anyone in the States. My sister had given me the phone number of a fella who was the ex-husband of a girl she worked with. I gave him a call and he let me stay at his place the first night. He knew someone who was renting a room – and away we go. The first couple of years were very difficult, homesick, the usual stuff, but then you get used to it, and there were certainly more opportunities in the States. I'm doing ok, I've worked for the same medical device company for the last fifteen years and am the Vice President of the company, not bad coming from the flats.

'This photo was taken in the backyard behind the Iveagh Baths (1980s). Barry Freer is on the left and Michael Kerfoot is on the right. The photo was taken by my mam'. Photo and caption courtesy of Andrew Kerfoot.

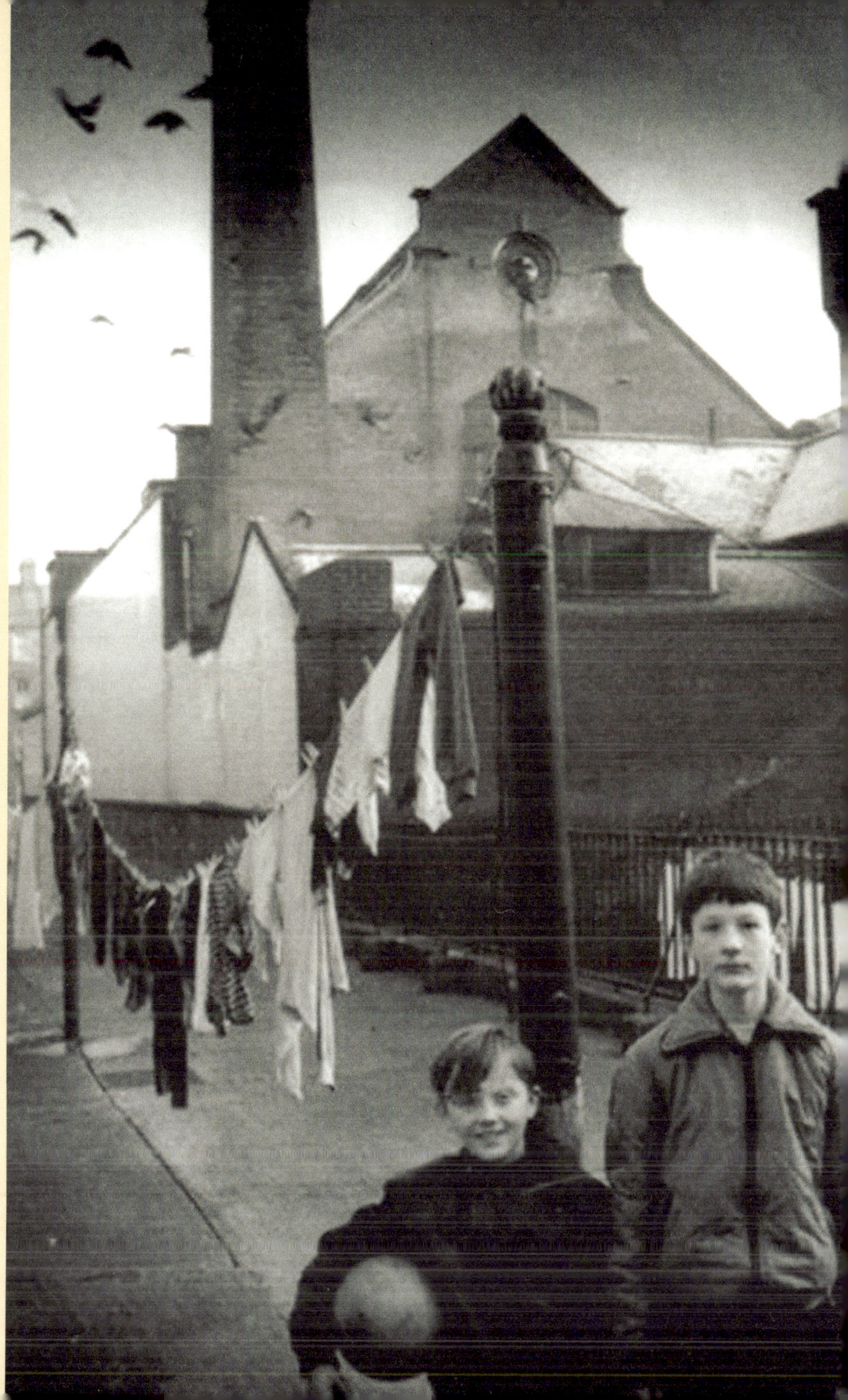

19

90s

Ross Road, 1993. The old back entrance to Henshaw's. The yard within the railings lay empty and unused for many decades and is still so to this day (see page 210). Photo courtesy of Carol Keogh.

■ Residents of Bride St in the heart of Dublin's Liberties still have to endure Dickensian living conditions that have nothing to do with "the rare old times".

THE FLATS WHERE TIME STOOD STILL

Why is this being done to us? Why are we being left out?

136/158 Hand-me-downs

It never really opened again. The Iveagh Market. It didn't, which is a shame. It's a fabulous building inside. The ground floor had all the vegetables, the fish. I used to remember Tony Matthews and the father, they sold meat and the Bernards they lived on the Ross Road and they sold all the vegetables and you went the other way and that was all the fish and you came back the other way and that's where Joe was and on the other side there was another butchers, I don't know their name. Oh God they're dead and buried. I'd say he's dead and buried now, I wouldn't say. I'm fifty-eight. Joe then must have been in his late thirties but a lovely man, lovely people and then upstairs was where they sold all the clothes, furniture all second hand, and hats. Now you'd see loads like of the elite that would be from the theatre – they'd all go and buy their clothes and their hats. They'd all buy their stuff there and they had all like say if you bought a coat they'd alter, the same with the hat. They had a milliners. You'd buy it from her and she'd charge you then for the alterations as well and that lady Molly would take them up and do everything with the coats.

People wore second-hand then and to pass down clothes was very common as well, like I remember getting me cousin's Confirmation coat and me granny turned the collar. It was a velvet collar. They passed them down. My sisters and I got my cousins. We went down like and we'd be getting altered and they used to cut the coats like, cut a piece off the coat and put velvet in it and then sew them back on. I mean they had great ideas, like.

137/158 The Swimmer

I learnt to swim in the Iveagh Baths. There was also the baths in Tara Street, the Guinness pool up in James's Street, which was solely for Guinness workers. People also swam in the canal among the dead cats! There was no hot water in the Iveagh Baths as well as... there was a shower area, but there wasn't hot. I was just thinking this morning, I got a man dead out in Seapoint, I was only about eighteen or nineteen, out there, in November it was, I used to cycle out on me bike, and swim, you know, and got a drowned man. He was way out, three or four hundred yards, somebody pointed him out, the man had a heart attack. There was nobody in the water except me, me and him, and I got him. I always liked swimming, but I was never coached.

A section from a newspaper article that documents conditions in the flats prior to their refurbishment (1997–2000). The picture shows May Murtagh, a member of the Residents Committee at this time. Evening Press, Monday, May 31, 1993.

Thirty Years After

I'm working up around the Rathgar area and he lived in one of the cul-de-sacs. My friends and I were working outside his door. I might have a bad memory for names but I never forget a face. I remembered him from thirty years ago – a teacher from my old school. I'm sitting looking at him and he's coming out of his house and he couldn't get out. The concrete is only being putting in. Me foreman Tony says, 'Run over and put a plank down there for that man to get out.' I swear to God he had a magnificent blue pin-striped suit and a gorgeous kind of a mauve tie. Me old memories are going three hundred miles an hour, thinking back to that time. That's the auld devil that murdered my brother with the pointer. So I ran across, I said, 'Excuse me, I'll be with you in a minute – just stay where you are bud I'll get you a plank.' I went and found one and laid it over the path and stepped away. 'Come on brother, you're all right,' and he takes his hat off, steps on the plank, scratching his head like he was trying to think where he knew me from. He missed a step, topples over and straight into the concrete he went. I said, 'Excuse me, are you okay there sir?' I said to him. 'Are you alright sir, come on and I'll help you up.' He said, 'Do I know you?' 'Well,' I said, 'you may have a short memory but my memory is long.' He said 'What do you mean?' 'Let me enlighten you,'

says I, 'I'll take you back to when I was eleven or a little older than eleven and you were beating the daylights out of my brother in the classroom because he didn't do his exercise.' And you'd think a bolt of lightning had hit him. 'It's .... isn't it?' he said. 'Yes sir it is,' I said, and me being the gentleman I am, I put me hand down and said, 'By the way sir, you were right, I only got a job on the Corporation.' 'Oh,' he said 'I heard it all now,' he says, 'By the way,' he says, 'do you want to come in for a drink?' I said, 'No thanks. No thanks sir,' I said, 'I don't drink on the job.' He said 'I must commend your memory, you have a wonderful memory.'

139/158 Regret

I do regret the problems I had in school because when my children were coming up it was an embarrassment to me when I had me son asking me what's that big word there or asking me to do a big long sum and I couldn't do it. I used to say, 'Look it son, ask mammy' and it was embarrassing to me. I felt that I'm not helping me kids though I should be helping me kids. I wasn't there for me own children like, you know what I mean. And other people say, 'Why didn't you go back to school?' Go back to school for what? I'm working in the Corporation, I'm in a rut.

140/158 New Flat

The baby came unexpectedly. We were living in this big one bed-roomed place. It was terrible, and damp, it was a policeman that owned it. It was very expensive, 105 pounds a week. We were sharing a toilet on the hallway with a refugee family, Kosovans and a Nigerian family. It wasn't well kept, the bathroom. And we had just had our child, and my partner was from quite a well-off family. I was embarrassed because we are in this situation – the place we had was not up to the standard. I said to her, 'How do you feel about going for a Corporation place?' and I saw these places being done up.

So I went into the Corporation and as I said this was now territory to me, I didn't know how you even applied. I filled in a form and they told me they would come out and see me and I would be assessed within six weeks. So I got a maximum situation because there was a baby. Because we were sharing a toilet and there was all these things. It took another six months after the

Names of past tenants engraved into the bricks of Bride Street. They trace a social and family history of their own. Photo by Chris Reid.

1990s

assessment. There was another issue with them, a very strong issue. 'Have you ever been on methadone?' They asked. The reason they asked that because if they asked 'Have you ever taken drugs or are you a drug addict?' Most people are going to say no. And I wrote I was on methadone. And I was on methadone at the time and I had been a drug user, but I was clean apart from my methadone. It was looking good, and we had the right amount of points. My situation wasn't bad. I was on the methadone and I did have a good record of clean urine and letters from the doctor saying I was clean – one thing supported the next. So I was told to tell the truth. It was in my best interests. So I decided to go with that. Kind of half sorry that I did. Because if you say you are on methadone, the ears all prick up. So I told them yes, I was clean and luckily enough I had a history of clean urine. I had six months clean urine and the man said 'Well you should have a year clean urine.' And I tried to explain that I had been away and I had broken the methadone treatment not because I had gone back on drugs, but because I went away. Just stopped going to the clinic and just self-medicated for a while. But the long and the short of it was, we got the flat. We got to move in together, the three of us. It was great. We hadn't got a thing and we had one mattress and two plastic chairs and a cardboard box. That was the first night. I just remember it, we were real excited. And we loved it you know. And we painted the flat.

Bronze Plaque installed on Bride Street. Story no. 140/158. See no. 8 on page 8 and 9. Photo by Chris Reid.

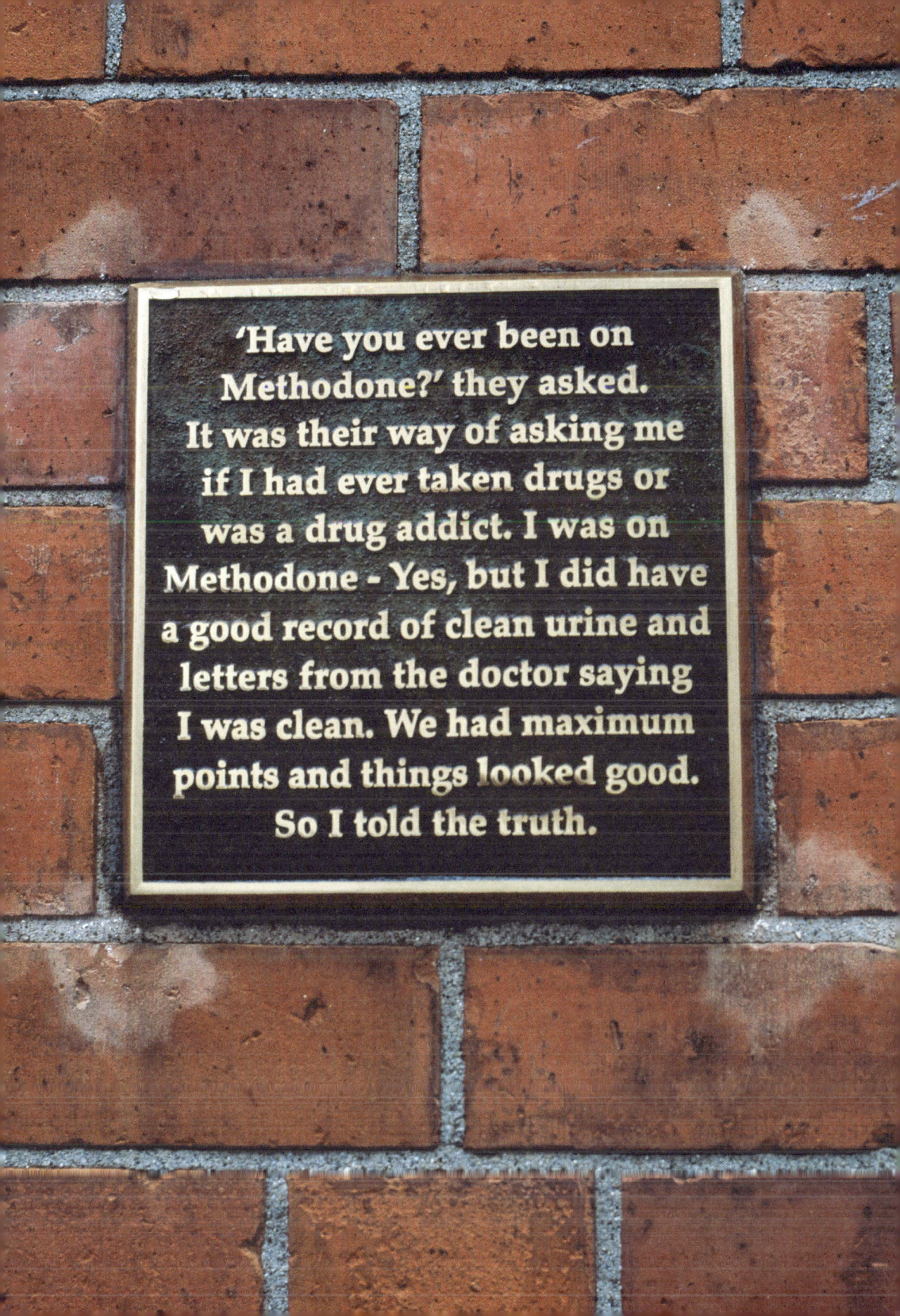

'Have you ever been on Methodone?' they asked. It was their way of asking me if I had ever taken drugs or was a drug addict. I was on Methodone - Yes, but I did have a good record of clean urine and letters from the doctor saying I was clean. We had maximum points and things looked good. So I told the truth.

An archaeological dig took place behind the flats on the Ross Road before they were renovated. Photos courtesy of Kieran Kavanagh, Dublin City Architects Division.

Up until the refurbishment that began in 1997, the yards to the flats were open and accessible to all (early 1990s). Photo courtesy of Kieran Kavanagh, Dublin City Architects Division.

20

196　Jason Keogh (left) visiting the corner shop, Bride Street, 2006. Photo by Chris Reid.

00s

2000s

141/158 Refurbishment

They just left the outside as a shell and gutted the whole inside of it and then refurbished it. And as I was saying they have intercoms and stuff like that and I know people that still live there. And the people were moved while this was going on. Now they could have been moved permanently if they wanted but very few of them did and they wanted to go back. If you look at the 1911 Census you'll see all those names, going back then and many of the names are still around that area like the descendants, so. I have known people who have moved out of the Liberties and moved back in a few weeks, because they couldn't get on 'out in the sticks' as they call it. All the people that I grew up with are still around anyway.

142/158 I Don't Know Anyone Now

They were so long renovating, I lost me husband and me mother, when we were waiting to move around to these flats. My mother picked out these two flats herself, she used to say, 'Now we'll go over to that new flat, you take one, I'll take the other.' She had these, so when she did die, I said, 'I don't care, I'll still take the flats that she had in it.'

Nicholas Street, 2006. Photo by Chris Reid.

I mean I don't know anyone on the Ross Road now. Me Da he had no recognition at all. An awful lot of people died, while waiting. There's only I'd say about ten old people that would remember it, the way it was before it was done up. An awful lot, they waited, you know, it was kind of too late for their times. Now it's a different generation, and everyone kind of keeps to themselves, it's not the same generation now, what it was years ago, although years ago, I suppose, people were more, they hadn't got money, do you know what I mean, money was scarce, but they were neighbours, and you opened your door, and you went in, and they always knocked to see were you alright, and you'd stand, and you'd have a chat. Everything has changed.

I Like It

There was no seats or anything, just a backyard. I mean it's kind of a little landscape now but before it was just a rough yard with bins everywhere. The kids used to play but it was very unhealthy but now it's quite nice, it's all landscaped with little seats there for people to sit on if they want to and they also gave us a balcony on the back where we don't have to go out to the yards, we can sit on our own balcony. It's quite nice now, you know. I like it very much – we have central heating. We've luxury now that we never had. I mean we have hot water with the turn of the tap.

Renovated yard behind the Bride Street end of the Ross Road. Photo by Chris Reid.

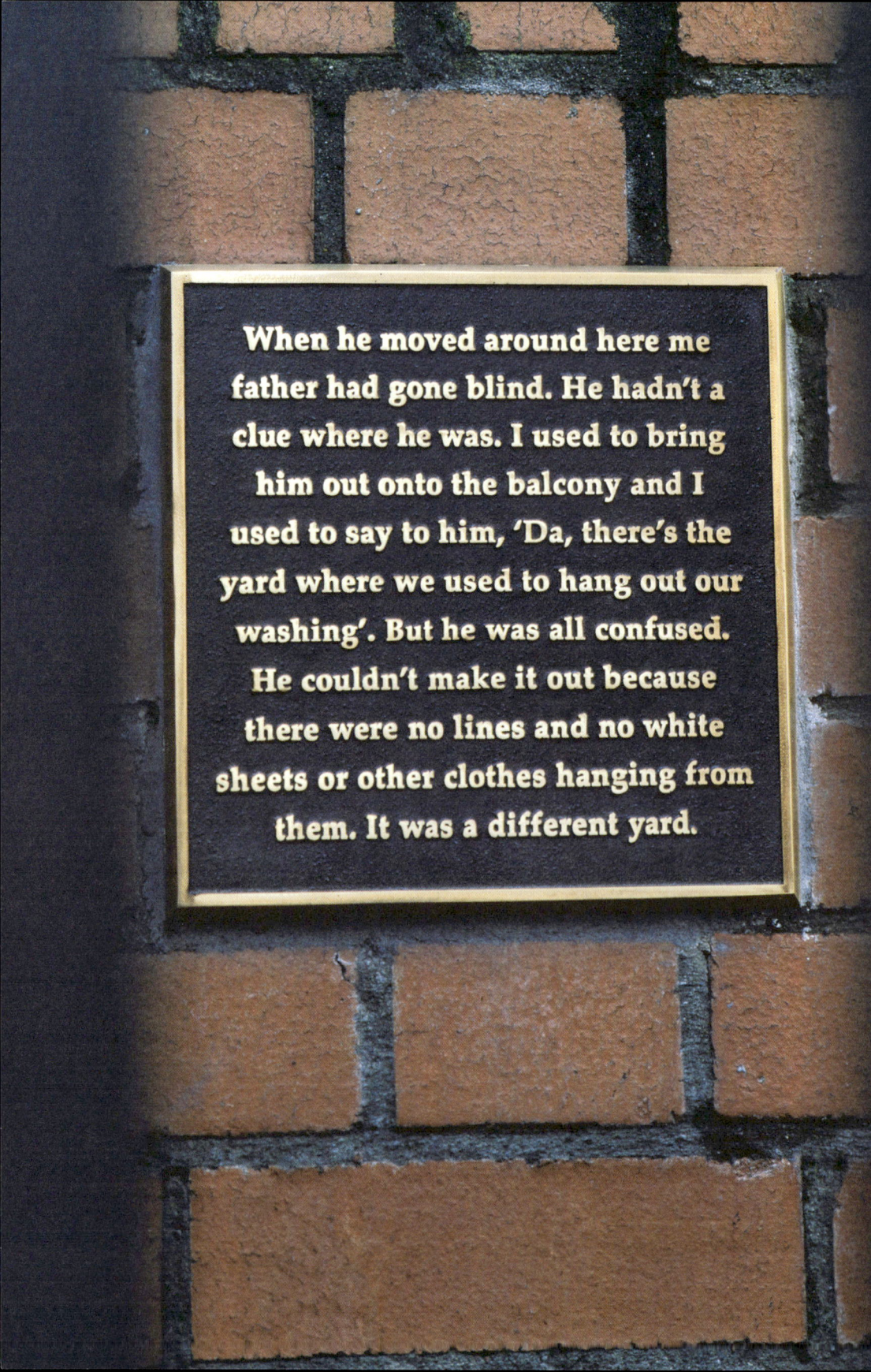

When he moved around here me father had gone blind. He hadn't a clue where he was. I used to bring him out onto the balcony and I used to say to him, 'Da, there's the yard where we used to hang out our washing'. But he was all confused. He couldn't make it out because there were no lines and no white sheets or other clothes hanging from them. It was a different yard.

New Yards, New Flats

When the flats were being renovated my father lost his sight. I used to bring him out on the balcony, and I used to say to him, 'Daddy, look it,' because when I'd be hanging out the washing, I lived next door to me Ma and Da all the time, when I first got married I lived in the next hall to them, and I'd say to him, 'Da, there's the yard where we used to hang out our washing,' but he was all confused, but he couldn't make it out because there was no lines, it was a different yard, you know what I mean.

I think it put an awful lot of pressure on old people, like their nerves all went and all, when they realised they had to move, but an awful lot of them died before the flats. To see the flats, I think it should have been done a long time ago, not only five years ago, it should have been done a long time ago for the people.

Local Pubs, Places, People

Me neighbours – I knew most of them and I actually ended up drinking in the same pub that me father drank in and my son drinks there now. It's next door to St. Audoen's church in the High Street and just around the corner from Nicholas Street. And they were all from that area, Nicholas Street, Ross Road, Bride Road, Bride Street and all around there. And people who I went to school with and I went to school in Cook Street, that is off Winetavern Street there. And we all knew each other and everyone in the Liberties knows each other. Like because you are going back there are good few schools in that area and we all went to school with each other, you know. There's something about the neighbourly thing in the Liberties plus the wit and the sense of humour with people. It's renowned for it and I don't know if it's only in the Liberties or it goes further afield, but it is definitely very common you know. Especially if you drink and I don't drink now and I haven't drank for years. But you would never be stuck for a pint. Put it that way.

The thing about the people from the Liberties is that no one ever sees wrong in other people. If they are up or they are down they will be helped by someone, you know. That is the way I found it anyway growing up there and looking back on it anyhow.

Bronze Plaque installed on Ross Road. Story no. 144/158. See no. 19 on page 8 and 9.
Photo by Chris Reid.

I'd be standing in the kitchen cooking my breakfast. I'd pull up the blinds and open the window to let air in. Next thing you see someone gawking in, waving in and taking snaps. Hello, one says. How are you sir? Good, I says. Would you like a rasher sandwich?

> We could have moved somewhere else. But why? We have been here so long that this is our home.

146/158 Home

So there's just two of us left, my sister died three years ago, she had got a flat around the corner here, on the Ross Road, you know, this is how it came about, that we're still here. When they were renovating these flats, we could have moved somewhere else, you know, but I said, 'Why bother now at this stage,' you know, we've been here so long that this is our home. So anyway they decided to do that side of the street first, that block over there, and Nicholas Street. So when they were finished they wanted to do here, so we had to move out, so because we didn't want to move away, they gave us a flat over there in No. 2 Hall, that's the first hall here on the corner. So then when these were finished, we could have stayed there, but we were on the third floor, so I said, 'Ah no, we've been here so long, this is our home, we'll go back to our own one,' you know, so we came back here, so this is where we've been ever since.

147/158 Familiar Foot, Strange Foot

It's only in latter years it kind of got noisy. I'd say in the nineties, but even in Nicholas Street people would go in and out and leave the hall door open. They weren't supposed to leave the door open. Years ago the door would be open and you felt pretty safe but you couldn't do it now – you'd be afraid if you heard someone coming up the stairs, you know, because every footstep on the stairs is kind of familiar. I know the family upstairs, I know their footsteps going up and I know who's coming down but when the hall door is left open at night if there's a strange foot it would be a bit scary. You get to know everyone, even their footstep. You can also tell the difference whether they're going up or down the stairs. You can even tell the difference in the children's footsteps…

148/158 After The Renovation

When my father came around to it too, he was after losing his sight, and like all these flats was done up, what happened was, my niece took him for the day, when we were moving around here, so he left the Ross Road, God help him, in the morning, and he was brought back to Bride Street in the night, and he'd be sitting there, and he'd say, 'I'm going to bed, good night' and he'd go in the kitchen, because he always slept in the front bedroom he was so

Previous Pages – Left: Bronze Plaque installed on Nicholas Street. See no. 2 on page 8 and 9. Right: Bronze Plaque installed on Bride Street. Story no. 146/158. See 11 on page 8. Photos by Chris Reid.

confused, you know what I mean, it took him an awful long time to kind of get into that routine, it was so confusing.

"I used to go to the Bird Market on Bride Street as a child. I'm sixty seven now. The Bird Market is every Sunday morning. I go every second or third week to buy and sell birds. Originally I'm from Saint Etna's Road in Cabra. I've been in Cabra all my life." Caption Courtesy of Christopher O'Flaherty. Photo by Chris Reid.

$\frac{149}{158}$ Refuge

Anyway I fell back into drugs, and the only comfort I got was from taking drugs, from someone who wasn't naturally turned on by them, I found a refuge in them, and it was another fuckin' ten years till I told my family, you know, I didn't tell them until after I'd moved home. I only told my family then, when I came home, I'd developed an addiction, you know. All the things I'd wanted, having a bit of a future, the things I'd wanted to do, the travelling I wanted to do, I wanted to have children, very much so, I thought that wasn't an option any more, I thought relationships were out of the question because of my health. I've been proved wrong though, as it evolved. I've been very lucky in that department, I don't know why, because I didn't really feel I had anything to offer her, at that stage, because when my addictions snowballed, you know, and my health got a little worse. I suppose they were all a bit fucked up, all the girls I met, I suppose they'd have to be, to kind of latch on to someone who's got so many issues, but I was lucky I did meet them, and had some very loving experiences, through just being in the situation, because I always told everyone, I was always up front about where I was at and it did nip a few things in the bud.

It's about twenty years I've got it now, I never thought I would see forty. I've probably more hope now, than I had then, which is crazy, I wasted twenty fuckin' years worrying about not living long enough, so because of that I said to myself this year, 'I'm forty, I never thought I would see forty.' Otherwise I would have done college years ago, you know, at least I'm doing something, because I could be here in five years time, maybe not very well, but I could be still here in five years time, and have fuck all done.

$\frac{150}{158}$ Misunderstanding

The upside is it's so central. The apartments are well sound. The maintenance is not very good, it's a joke really. There's people here, they have a great sense of their history but there isn't a good sense of community. People just have this negative outlook on things when you ask them to get involved in community to improve maintenance. They say it's not going to do any good anyway. They never done anything for us in the past. But what they did do was they renovated the place and that was over seven years ago and what they don't do is maintain and if you don't maintain something, it's going

Bronze Plaque installed on Ross Road. Story no. 150/158. See no. 15 on page 8 and 9. Photo by Chris Reid.

The renovation was completed in September 2000. But if you don't maintain a place it will fall into disrepair and over time the people living there will become demoralised. The place will then go back to the way it was before.

2000s

to fall into disrepair and people will also get fed up with the fact that this place is not being maintained. I got involved in a committee in the community development initiative here to get people's voice heard and it was like pulling teeth and then they're very suspicious about you when you are. They think you're a vigilante or something. I think someone over there said it. What we're trying to do is have people do their job. I got involved in a committee in the community development area so as to put pressure on people to provide a service, which is necessary in order for people to feel secure in their homes and get a good sense of community.

Renovated yard behind Bride Road and Bride Street flats. Photo by Chris Reid.

Drugs

When I was young and free and wild
Twas Mams and Dads were mourned by child
But drugs have turned these things around
Now Mam's and Dad's put child in ground
Walking thought my Dublin Streets
My Dublin parks aswell
Where once there had been paradise
Has been replaced by hell
Kids with drugs they smoke or snort
A pusher on the corner like a poisoned wart
Oh where are all the boys and girls
That I ran with on these streets
Few did land on foregin shores
More lie beneath their withered wreaths
The Celtic tiger roared and roared
The rich got richer still
The men in suits they robbed us blind
As mothers wept in summer hill
Some men will live on the addict's woe
And laugh and count their gain
Mams and Dads will visit graves
Only heaven knows their pain
So now I'm heading for the countryside
To the rivers fields, and bogs
For drugs have ruined my Dublin town
Now it's going to the dogs

Poem by Leo Magee 09/03/2004

It would be good if a community centre could be built here. Even if one of the flats was put aside for it. Somewhere for the kids to go at night. It could be nice if some sort of football pitch could be built into one of the yards. Maybe more trees could be planted.

151/158 Relationship

What I'd want to do is bring about that kind of change, to have a relationship with City Council and that hasn't happened yet. I like this area because as I said it's so central. I like the people in it because it's the type of people I've grown up with, working class people, they have similar type values that I have and similar type of principles I've been brought up with. But it's not really like that now. A lot of people are more scared than they would have been. They don't know each other as much. It has potential but I don't think it's been reached. It has potential but a few things need to be addressed to secure part of the community, that the right services are available in particular play areas for the kids. Protection of their flats, more policing. We very, very seldom see police on this road, very seldom.

Jamie Doyle (left) and Jason Keogh (right) on Bride Street, 2006. Photo by Chris Reid.

Bronze Plaque installed outside the old back entrance into Henshaw's (see page 186) on the Ross Road. See no. 17 on page 8 and 9. Photo by Chris Reid.

2000s

152/158 Dublin 2 or Dublin 8?

I was involved locally but packed it in because I told them if they didn't vote in the next election, that I was out. During that election I went and I looked at the register, I was the last to vote, right, I left it to the last minute, I said if people didn't bother their arse coming out and voting I was out of it, and that was it. So they didn't, so I left it, I was fed up wasting me time, you know. Another problem is we're on this street – it's part of the Local Authority, right. This is Dublin 8 here, but for Dáil Elections we're part of the other side, Dublin 2. It's very weird when you're trying to get politicians to do something for you, you know, it puts you at a disadvantage it does, a very big disadvantage. I suppose the boundaries have to be drawn somewhere, but it's really weird the way it fell here, you know.

Saint Patrick's Day, 2010. The parade passes through Nicholas Street each year. Photo by Chris Reid.

> "This place has a history. But it's also a living thing. We are living in the here and now" [13]

153/158 Living History

It has a history thing. It's not history, it's a living thing. We're living in the here and now. History they say, what are you talking about, d'ye know what I mean, so if you don't feel part of your community, you're going to be isolated when you don't have the services. There's a lot of depression and alcoholism and a lot of stuff manifests itself and all that stuff, all the years of people failing in their response to provide the necessary services for people. I come from a family, eleven children and under stress, alcoholism, poverty, all that stuff. You don't come away unscathed through that. I managed to look at my sense of self and I know I have a sense of history and I know I have a sense of value.

154/158 Grateful

I have heard this back from the local corner shop and I don't know how true this is, but the person who had this flat was the friend of the one downstairs that I have never got on with, until recently, right. And she was moved out to the flats across the road and when these were done up and she saw her friend's flat, she wanted to move back but my partner and myself were here at the time. It was resentment from the woman downstairs and that her friend couldn't have her flat back.

I am very lucky to have it but I think I deserve it because I am so grateful for it, if you know what I mean. I look after it and I love it. And I think if you really love something and you have it and no matter what it is, and you look after it then you deserve it. Because we are only caretakers for the things we have. That is the way I see life. And I think I take care of this the best I can, you know. I found when I went around and knocked on everyone's door, got them all to meet downstairs just to have a word and broke the ice with them they were all very open and welcoming. That woman downstairs was the initial thorn in my side here and didn't like me at all, and you know, accused me for all sorts of things. It took a long time but there is a good kind of thing there now, you know. She even popped up once to say I am going to England to see my sons for a couple of weeks and can you keep an eye on my flat. I gave her a bottle of sherry at Christmas.

13. See page 231

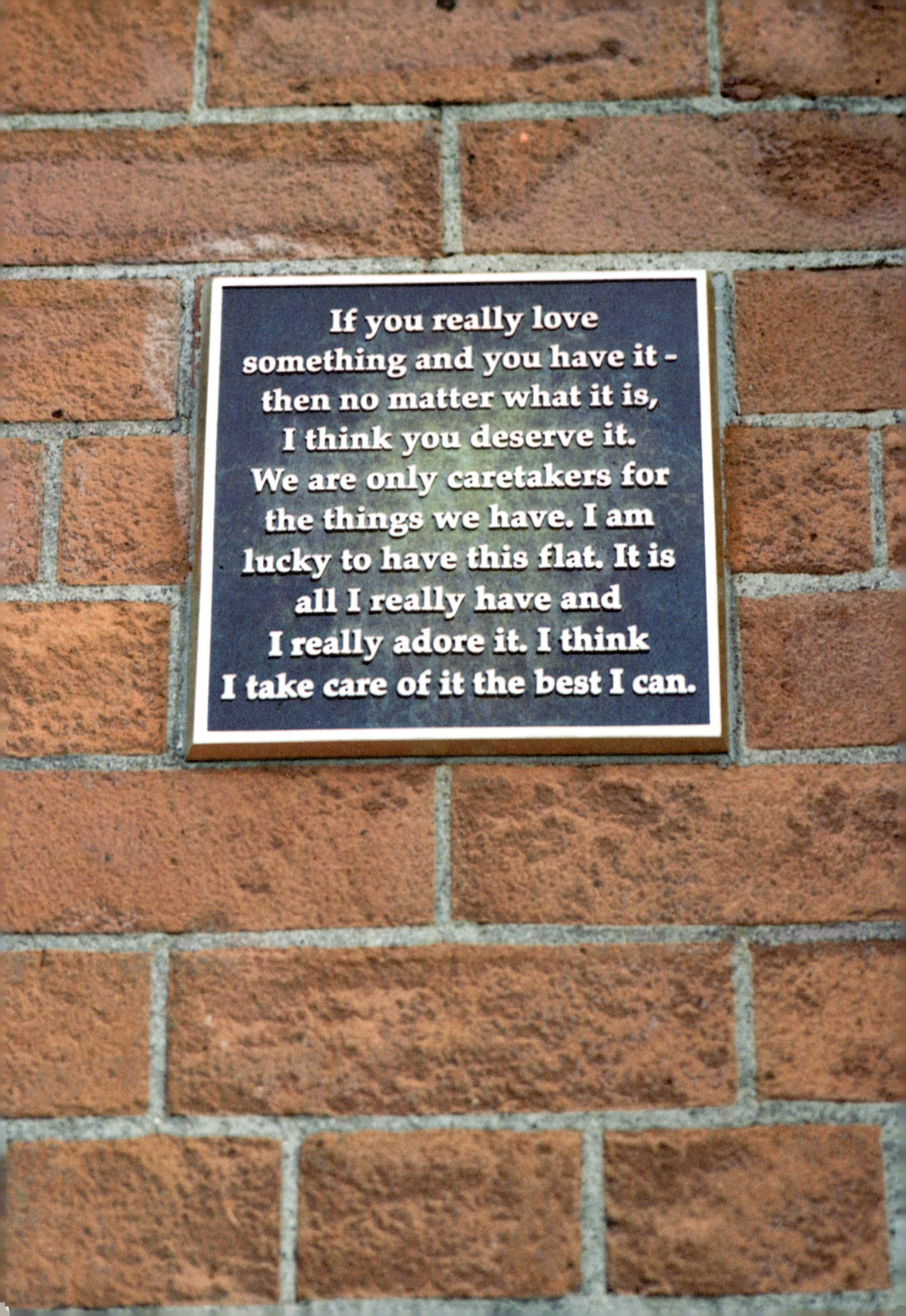

If you really love
something and you have it -
then no matter what it is,
I think you deserve it.
We are only caretakers for
the things we have. I am
lucky to have this flat. It is
all I really have and
I really adore it. I think
I take care of it the best I can.

$\frac{155}{158}$ Looking Back, Looking Forward

People were accepting of things in those days – just lived from day to day, they had no power, no personal motivation. When you're a kid you don't notice it. Only afterwards you realise it. Things are different now, you wouldn't put up with the kind of things you had to put up with years ago. It's not the most pleasant of things. It could have been better. And kids have it better now. Because they do have a sense of personal power, you know they have rights, then they had no rights, none.

I don't particularly want to know about the past myself really because it's just an unsatisfactory part of your life in a lot of ways. When you got old enough the way forward in the future is the only thing to look for. To move away from all that. I moved out from all that, got away from it. It's not the same and you are not the same, you are not a child anymore.

Left: Bronze Bronze Plaque installed on Nicholas Street. Story no. 154/158. See no. 4 on page 8 and 9. Above: Bride Street, 2006. Photos by Chris Reid.

Aidan Walsh, of the Ross Road prepares for Christmas. Courtesy of Aidan Walsh. aidanwalshdublin@gmail.com. www.aidanwalsh.com. Photo by Aidan Walsh and Chris Reid.

$\frac{156}{158}$ I'm Fairly Happy But . . .

I've six lovely kids and they're all grown up now. I've actually got five grandchildren. Me recent one was only Monday, a lovely little girl. They're good kids like, you know, but it's very hard to get them motivated – they keep telling me I'm old fashioned. My latest grandchild was born last Monday. She was 7lbs 7. She was gorgeous. But I have two beautiful grandchildren a boy and a girl of five and the other two, one is two and the other is two the month after in March. But they're beautiful kids. I feel sorry for meself sometimes because I didn't push meself. Not just work. I mean education and getting a better job. I'm sorry I didn't do something more with my life but I'm fairly happy. I often tell me own children, Don't follow in your father's footsteps. Don't make the same mistakes as me. Go back to school for a couple of years. Take up a plastering course . . .

157/158 Archaeology

They didn't build on the site directly after the tenement collapsed in 1941 (see page 63) because you see they had to get rid of the building that fell, then the next one was 45 and the next one 44 was a double house but they were all condemned then when that happened. Later Donnelly's was there, a garage. That's only recently closed. They demolished it in 2008. The archaeologists were in there. I used to pass by and say to them, 'Did you find my mother's rings. They was buried in there'. But they didn't know what I was talking about. They were from the country; sure they wouldn't know anything about it. They only went there to work on the foundations. They were going to build a new police station there, then the boom stopped, they stopped, the building stopped.

158/158 The Balconies

Often I'd go out on me balcony, and I'd look over, and I would say to meself 'now if my Ma lived there, my Ma would be standing on that balcony, and their next door neighbour Mrs. Forte, would be sitting there, and Mrs. Connaughton would be there, and Mrs. Dalton would be there, Mrs. Byrne would be there, Mrs. Kelly would be there'. That was the six tenants that lived up the hall. That was No. 1 Ross Road, and I'd always be standing there, and maybe looking, and I can imagine all the people that lived there, standing out on them balconies now.

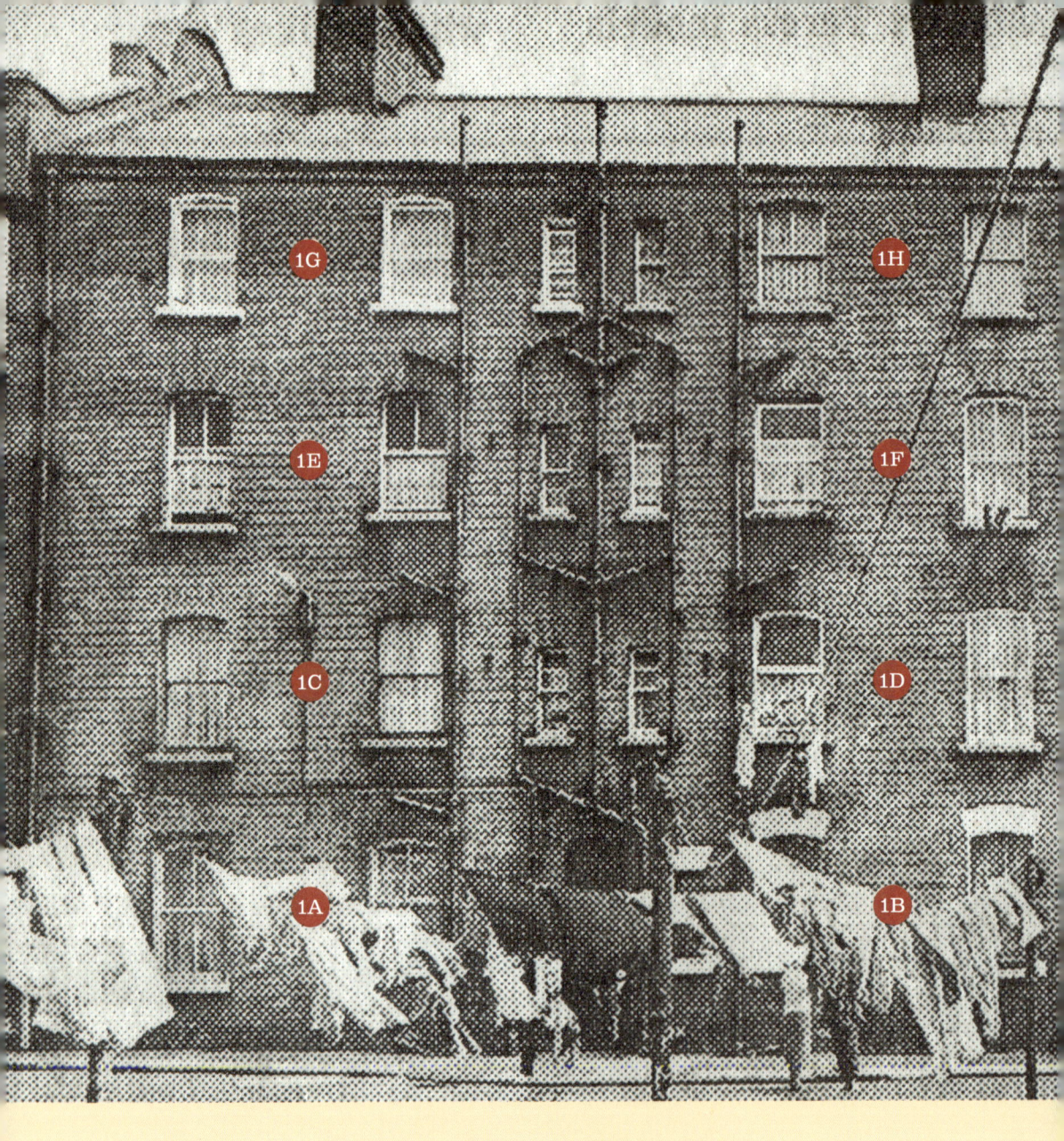

Some Past Residents

Some of the families who lived in hall 1 and hall 2 of old Bride Street from the 1940s and 1950s. Courtesy of Mary Murtagh.

1G. Greenes (Molly & Family)
1E. Kennys (Kevin, Matt, Granny)
1C. Farrells (Sissy, Kathleen, Patsy)
1A. Redmonds (Later Freers)

1H. Beckleys
1F. Doyles
1D. Neilans
1B. McFaddens
    Forsyths

2G. Dignams
2E. Cummins
2C. Dolly Rice
2A. Byrnes

2H. Kellys
2F. Bernards
2D. Flannagans
2B. Dorans

Photo published in The Evening Press on Monday 31st May 1993 with an article titled "The Flats Where Time Stood Still" (see page 188).

219

Figure and Ground: Reflections on the Practice of Chris Reid

Professor Declan McGonagle

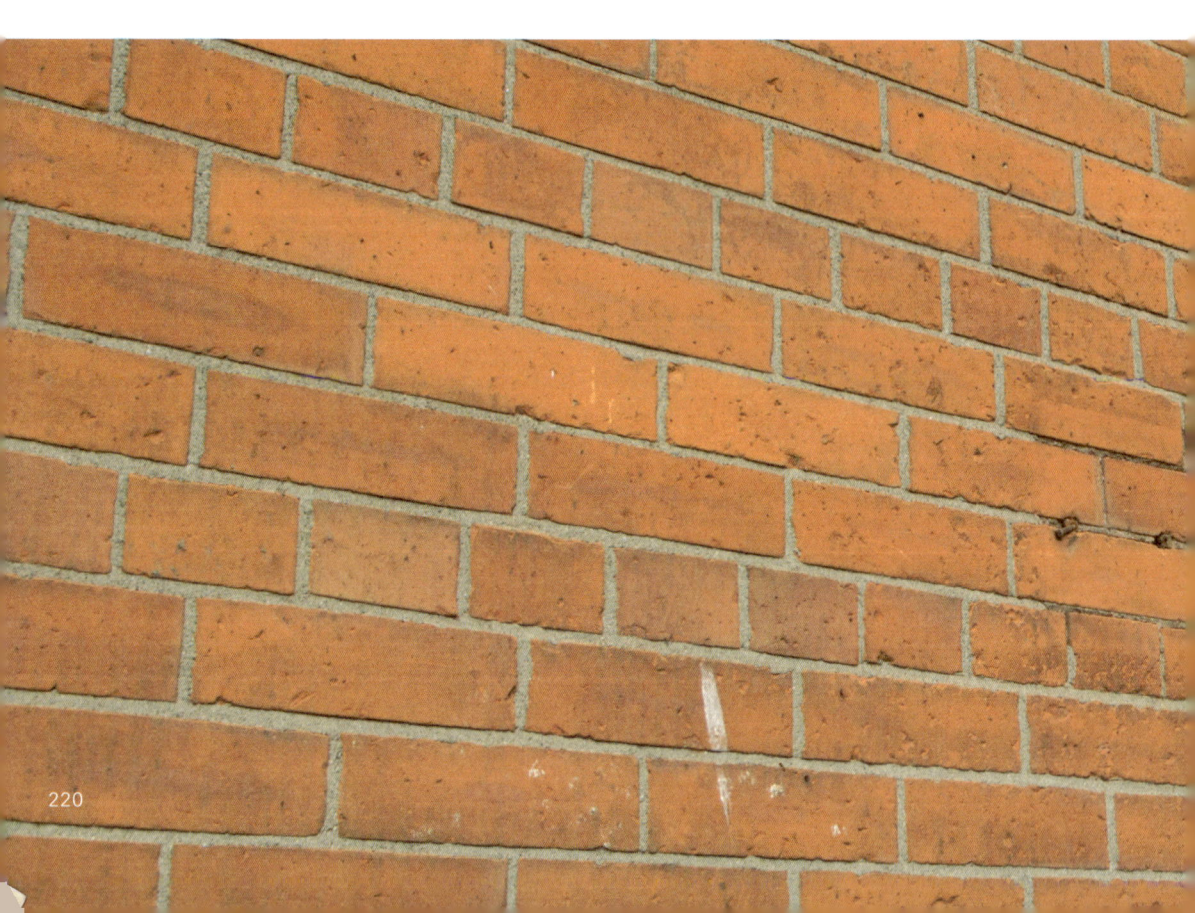

Chris Reid's practice as an artist embodies the idea that new forms of art and new procedures are necessary if a new set of relations is to be negotiated and sustained between artist and non-artist. There is a lot of work today which operates under the catch-all headings of socially engaged practice and relational practice which are all qualitatively different from previous ideas of Community Arts. In my view, much of this work is concerned with a *representation* of those proposed new relations rather than an *embodiment* of actual relationships in a field of practice. At the same time, we have to acknowledge that not all practitioners or those who mediate in the visual arts recognise that a new set of relations is necessary, or even desirable, and are content with the status quo. This contentment is expressed in not only forms of practice but also in the still dominant forms of distribution. This too is how Chris Reid's practice challenges inherited ideas of commodity and the setting of the exchange, transaction or negotiation with the non-artist. The traditional idea of viewer simply doesn't hold in relation to this work and the intentions behind it. I have come to know Chris Reid's work through direct experience of projects and through working with him on works in Dublin and Belfast. Typically, these projects use texts based on extensive interviews with people from geographically defined areas or in areas of human activity, with carefully edited sections of text – in some senses a fragment standing for the whole – inserted into public space, on a billboard scale or insinuated into public consciousness on a much more intimate scale. This often mimics the sort of heritage signage and historical plaques which mark historical sites and buildings in cities. It could almost be described as an art of insinuation. The carriers of the text, and therefore the meaning of the work, are so familiar to 'a reader' that their engagement is almost unconscious, until of course the text presents itself as a problematic and not as a resolved narrative. Advertising, a power in the public domain, works, as the Irish born media artist Les

Chris Reid putting the finishing touches on a plaque. Photo by Anthony Cassidy.

Levine has said, by creating anxiety and then proposing the means to resolve that anxiety. In Reid's work anxiety is created quietly but it is left unresolved. His work is, therefore, not object based at all, although it is carried materially on plaques, signs and familiar information systems on the street. Their very familiarity is part of their effect and their power. Reid's art operates in the transactional space between the text and the reader, whoever that is, and on the street it can literally be anybody, and is made and re-made each time it is experienced. This is a very powerful model of practice precisely because it works outside the received notions of art production and distribution to include the 'viewer' in the making of meaning. Far from being reduced by the process, the location and the procedures developed by Reid, amplify the experience of the art in situ. In his most recent project in Dublin 8 the procedure started with the act of knocking on people's doors and talking to them, not all of whom responded, understood or valued the process, but many did collaborate. In doing so it was interesting how many revealed an inner and outer life – an official and unofficial set of experiences – articulated in a sort of weave of narrative, incidents, memories, dreams and aspirations rolled into a single stream of communication. Our Western culture is guilty of understanding history as the collected narratives of the rich and powerful in society. Those whose lives are apparently worth documenting. Many historians over the last two to three decades have projected another reading of history based on the lives of the many rather than the few. We still live in a socio-political media space which celebrates and elevates the rich and powerful as admirable, and one of the measures of that power is also, of course, the capacity to collect works of art as commodities. The rich and powerful continue, even in leaner times, to use art to transform wealth into prestige and in doing so create a virtuous circle of attention around themselves.

What this work is really about is value and values. Those who are documented, especially in mass media space, are valued, but it is interesting that though Reid's work and strategy also involves documentation, it is not the same in form or intention as a tradition of say black and white documentary photography, which in the 20th century seemed to focus on the many, the street and the marginalised – to the point of cliché. Reid's documentation confers value on voice and the life as lived, not as observed by a supposedly innocent artist's eye.

The relationship between subject and object is complex and not at all innocent. In this work the ethical responsibilities of art are foregrounded over its aesthetic responsibilities. That is not to say that this work does not have an aesthetic proposition. Everything counts. The point size of the text, the size of the sign, how it is fixed to a wall or to railings, how it relates to the field of heritage and information signage are

A wall in the artist's studio in 2008 showing rough designs for plaques. Photo by Chris Reid.

Row 1

We could have moved somewhere else. But why? We have been here so long that this is our home.

locals w/ Historical

I'd be standing in the kitchen cooking my breakfast. I'd pull up the blinds and open the window to let air in. Next thing you see someone gawking in, waving in and taking snaps. Hello, one says. How are you sir? Good, I says. Would you like a rasher sandwich?

Tourism + locals

They had seven children and decided this was enough. One day after mass, she arrived home and told her husband that the priest said no one of childbearing age should stop having children. Sometime later she had another. Both she and the baby died during the birth. They were buried together.

Catholic Dogma

My Father was in the British Army during the 1st World War. He got some medals, but when he left the army he pawned them and never redeemed them. My brother, he was in the British Airforce during the 2nd World War. My Father was mad to know about it. He used to say to my mother. I can't get a word out of him. My brother got the Burma Star and all, but he never even wrote away for his medal. He said he didn't need medals to remind him

Wars w/ Past Gory

The hill was steeper, the street narrower. The surface was all cobblestones. When winter weather made them freeze, horses struggled to climb. Sparks flew from their hooves.

Row 2

My mother didn't believe in doctors. She couldn't afford to pay them anyway. All the mothers were the same. They had these old fashioned remedies. 'I'll cure you myself', my mother used to say.

+ Mothering

It was an issue with them. They asked me, 'Have you ever been on Methodone?'. This was their way of asking 'Have you ever taken drugs or were a drug addict?'. I was on methodone, yes, but I did have a good record of clean urine and letters from the doctor saying I was clean. **We** had maximum amount of points and things looked good. So I told the truth.

+ Who is We?
(Holy Family)

From the time I was born Moggs was there. I'd be swinging on the lamp post for scutting the back of the coal lorry and she'd be sitting there at the window her dog beside her, watching the kids and the people. She had six kids herself and she was left a young widow. She'd wash the dead or anything to earn a shilling to rear them and if she never had a shilling she was always in good form. She'd go around for a few glasses of stout at Corbetts and would come around singing.

Individual as historical

I never really had a conversation with my Father. Sometime in the 1960's he caught me mitching from school and gave me an awful hiding. Ripped the clothes off me, lashed me with the belt and punched me in the eyes.

HOW CHILDREN WERE TREATED

In 2008 the artist Chris Reid completed an artwork consisting of 20 bronze plaques and a printed book. The texts on the plaques and in the book are based upon transcripts of recordings the artist made of conversations he had with residents and people associated with Nicholas Street, Ross Road, Bride Street, and Bride Road between the years 2004 and 2008. The plaques were installed on the walls of these streets in 2008.

HOLD
art project

Row 3

There was six tenants up the hall and every neighbour would wash their flight down to the next woman underneath them and that woman would come out and wash the steps to the next one and so on. Everyone took their turn to wash the stairs and all.

COMMUNITY WAYS

[redacted/blurred text]

During the 1980's there was still no hot water in the flats. I had to go round to the Iveagh for a bath. I'd paid a few pence and go upstairs. There were seperate rooms where you had your bath. I'd go mostly of a saturday. By times I'd meet people who were in the same predicament as myself.

Iveagh Baths

They did renovate the place. But if you don't maintain the place it will fall into disrepair and over time the people living there will become demoralised. The place will then revert back to the place it was before the renovation.

Renovation, maintenance resilient

'Rags, rags, rags', he'd shout. The Ragman was a fella on a horse and cart, he'd have goldfish in little jars. He'd give you one if you brought down a good clover coat or some other article. Sometimes me Da noticed things missing and he'd lose the head. The Ragman always came of a Friday or Saturday morning - right, when he'd know your parents would be working or out getting messages. He'd come of a Tuesday as well because he'd know the women would be up washing their clothes in the wash house by the Iveagh market. He stopped coming around in 1967

RAG+BONE MAN

Row 4

There was a toss school of a Sunday. Men would gather behind the Iveagh Baths which was our back yard. They'd have notes and coins in a pot on the ground in the middle of them. Side bets were taken as well. If you seen the cops coming you ran over shouting, 'Cops! Cops!', and the men all ran off. Occasionally I'd do that just to get the few bob left on the ground. The cops would be coming up the yard and they'd ask, 'What are you doing?' 'I'm hanging out the washing', I'd say and shake out the tea towel I kept over my shoulder.

Toss school

I ended up drinking in the same pub me Father drank in. The main thing in the small pubs was the camaraderie, people helping each other, the sing-song, the sense of humour. If you were looking for a fella to do something you wouldn't go to his house, you'd go to the pub. You'd ask where he drinks not where he lives. Many are gone now such as O'Byrnes, O'Connells, Napper Tandy, Corbetts, Graces, Phelans

Place of Pub + Culture

I am lucky to have this flat but I think I deserve it because I am so grateful for it. I look after it and love it. I think if you really love something and you have it and no matter what it is then you deserve it. Because we are only caretakers for the things we have. This flat is all I really have and I really adore it. I think I take care of this the best I can.

There was a chemical factory across the road. It went up in flames in the 1940's. It blazed for three days. They levelled it and turned it into a car park. My father worked there. Later they built flats on it.

changes in environment + local jobs

He had no family. He had a stick because of his wooden leg. He would stand at the railings and he would be shaking. He would shout. He would bang the railings and bang the ground with his stick. You would hear the clanging. He would wave his stick around or raise the stick in mid-air. Then he started to swipe at people. That is how it effected him - the war.

LOCATION: in middle of GABLE END

DUBLIN MEMORIES
ORMOND ROAD, SOUTH

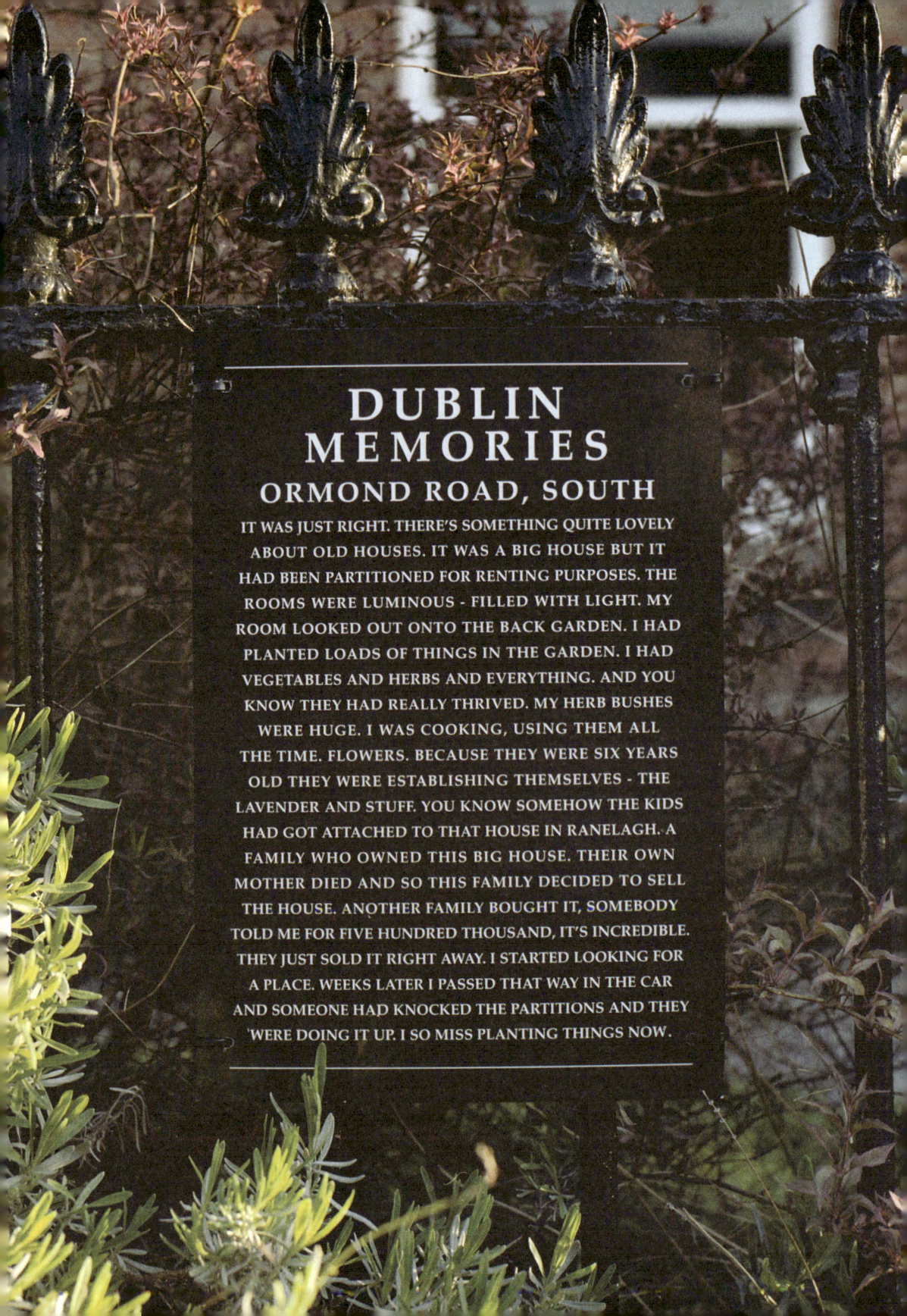

IT WAS JUST RIGHT. THERE'S SOMETHING QUITE LOVELY ABOUT OLD HOUSES. IT WAS A BIG HOUSE BUT IT HAD BEEN PARTITIONED FOR RENTING PURPOSES. THE ROOMS WERE LUMINOUS - FILLED WITH LIGHT. MY ROOM LOOKED OUT ONTO THE BACK GARDEN. I HAD PLANTED LOADS OF THINGS IN THE GARDEN. I HAD VEGETABLES AND HERBS AND EVERYTHING. AND YOU KNOW THEY HAD REALLY THRIVED. MY HERB BUSHES WERE HUGE. I WAS COOKING, USING THEM ALL THE TIME. FLOWERS. BECAUSE THEY WERE SIX YEARS OLD THEY WERE ESTABLISHING THEMSELVES - THE LAVENDER AND STUFF. YOU KNOW SOMEHOW THE KIDS HAD GOT ATTACHED TO THAT HOUSE IN RANELAGH. A FAMILY WHO OWNED THIS BIG HOUSE. THEIR OWN MOTHER DIED AND SO THIS FAMILY DECIDED TO SELL THE HOUSE. ANOTHER FAMILY BOUGHT IT, SOMEBODY TOLD ME FOR FIVE HUNDRED THOUSAND, IT'S INCREDIBLE. THEY JUST SOLD IT RIGHT AWAY. I STARTED LOOKING FOR A PLACE. WEEKS LATER I PASSED THAT WAY IN THE CAR AND SOMEONE HAD KNOCKED THE PARTITIONS AND THEY WERE DOING IT UP. I SO MISS PLANTING THINGS NOW.

all features considered by the artist and acted upon in different ways in each different situation. To Chris Reid public space is actually public mind. How and why we see as well as what we see and also what we already know. His interviews draw out from those who take part, extraordinary statements and points of view. A project in Belfast in 2006 involved interviews about the 'Troubles' and the day to day life in the face of actual or possible violence in areas of the city. To have people talk openly demonstrates another dimension of the artist's practice and that is the issue of time. It is not simply a matter of working slowly and carefully, but how time is one of the key planks of meaning in this practice. Time spent on reconnaissance and research, time spent on establishing contacts, on building trust to an extraordinary degree and also the time it takes to establish more formal supports for the realisation of any specific project. The conversations/interviews which took place were allowed to take their own course. In the Dublin 8 project, the trust, once built up, allowed for an expansive report on a life, and lives lived, in a small number of streets in the Dublin 8 area. This is a kind of history that is not only about the many, it is also owned by the many. It is their possession, and in the immediacy of that part of the city, that ownership, still held in common over generations, subverts the usual power relationships which operate in relation to specific parts of Dublin and any city. Too often people from certain identified areas of cities like Dublin, do not participate in the social process, except in certain predetermined marginalised or outsider roles and appear almost to be eavesdropping even on their own realities. That is the nature of powerlessness. It internalises a disbelief of worth and value in self, in relation to those who have social, cultural and economic power. If Chris Reid's project is important as a model, it is because of the way it ventilates histories from within, brings them to the surface in public space and proposes that the chosen fragment of an interview – with a sense of voice and place – stand for a whole constellation of narratives that have meaning and value. These narratives are present universally but are classified by the socio-cultural processes that determine value and worth, which is, in effect, only a reflection of whether those narratives are attached to power – certain kinds of socio-economic power – or held apart from it. Classification is what the traditional model of museum was supposed to do. All human beings, as is evidenced in Reid's texts, make and do things to add value to the quality of their lives. Problems arise only when this making and doing is classified according to pre-defined concepts of value and worth which are then captured and reinforced by a variety of institutional and cultural models. Chris Reid's strategic practice cuts across all of these forms of art and institutional production, distribution and validation.

While it clearly helps to have institutional support, his practice is not dependent upon it, yet at the same time he is completely aware of the need to relate to the processes and procedures of the art world in order both to sustain his practice and to ensure

One of 35 plaques installed around Dublin City in May 2002. The plaques were made from black PVC. It was a temporary project and all the plaques were removed over time. Photo by Chris Reid.

One of a series of signs installed in Belfast, November 2006, as part of the 'I Confess That I Was There' exhibition at the Switch Room and other locations, Belfast. Photo by Chris Reid.

distribution of the ideas of another model of practice and another way of negotiating and inhabiting public space. By public space I mean that space which is shared with non-artists. While this can be defined as any public gallery/museum or institutional space, the ultimate challenge lies in negotiating that sharing in a way which does not diminish the practice, or patronise the publics who use the space. As a result, when the Chris Reid project is in situ and doing its work it is literally owned by those who have supplied the narratives but also by those who discover the texts and have an immediate experience and construct their own meaning from the work.

Chris Reid's work confronts Modernism and then by-passes it and operates within another space. It embodies a set of relations, independent of a narrowing debate about Modernism or Post-Modernism which is a constant in group discourse about art and its place in the world. As stated above, there are many who argue art has no role in the world, only in culture. That is a debate which Reid's work confounds. It is so clearly a product of the world where culture is not something that you possess but something you inhabit and which inhabits you. This is the figure and ground issue. Art history in traditional form has taught us that the Renaissance's great achievement was the separation of the figure from the Byzantine ground and the creation of pictorial space.

> I was managing a department that was responsible for the payments the company made. These payments were made everyday, in millions. The computer systems had to be working or our reputation would go down the tubes. I also felt responsible for some of the people who weren't coming up to scratch on our team. I worked late hours and took work home. After fourteen years, this anxiety over work got to me. It played havoc with my relationship. It came to a head just before Christmas. My wife and I were not speaking. She had gone out. I think she went shopping. Despite the freezing cold, I went out to make a garden path. I furiously dug, carried, mixed and laid cement for about five hours. I was hoping, praying something would happen. That I would get a heart attack or something. I wanted to get away from the pain. I wanted everything to be over. I went upstairs to the bedroom, where there were some pills. I swallowed them all and lay on the bed, exhausted. I don't know what happened, but the next day I woke. My wife didn't say anything about it. I can't remember how I got to a doctor.

City Quay Text, December 2002 – City Arts Centre.

Representations of that idea of the autonomy of the individual and the separation of the figure of the artist from the ground of community or the society is a Modernist idea which has occurred throughout human history when the idea that things happen as a result of the actions of man rather than (God) nature, was dominant. The result of this notion developing traction again over the last four hundred years i.e. from the Renaissance recovery of classical (modernist) humanist ideas – is the idea of the artist as a lone genius producer which is only partly being challenged in recent decades by other definitions of value.

What is interesting in relation to this sort of background debate to which Chris Reid as an artist is unavoidably connected is how, when challenging the orthodoxy of figure and ground, embodying a model or figure in the ground, the artist in this case does not surrender his autonomy at all. He manages to maintain a dynamic tension between his identity as a practitioner and the ground of community and context from which he draws meaning and to which he always returns value. It is this that I am proposing constitutes the innovation in Chris Reid's practice, not simply the change in material form or the change of location from gallery to street, but the shift in ideology about the nature and purpose of art making, why and for whom it is made in the first place.

Heirlooms & Hand-me-downs

The Plaques

These extracts were among 220 in total considered for inclusion on one of the final 21 plaques that now appear on the walls of buildings throughout Nicholas Street, Bride Street, Bride Road and the Rosser.

1.
Title: Father
Page: 18

2.
Title: What Your Mother Said Was Law
Page: 45

3.
Title: We Didn't Have Locks
Page: 46

4.
Title: Other People's Homes
Page: 47

5.
Title: They Passed Remarks
Page: 51

6.
Title: Net Curtains and White Sheets
Page: 60

7.
Title: The Telegram Boy
Page: 68

8.
Title: Games and Schools
Page: 85

1

He had a lot of chest trouble. He didn't have it before he went away. He was perfectly healthy and he came back with it. You'd want to hear him coughing. They hadn't him down as being gassed in the war. They say he died from shrapnel in his face and the loss of a little finger.

2

Those days were all so innocent. You weren't afraid to go down the street, or go anywhere or talk to anyone. We were let stay out to about eight O'clock. My mother wouldn't even let us stay in the house, because if we came up here she'd say 'What's wrong with you. Are you sick. Why are you not out playing. She wouldn't allow us to stay in all day especially if the weather was good. She'd say, 'Go out and enjoy God's sunshine.

3

There were no locks on the doors as such. A hole was bored into the door and a piece of twine was put through it.

4

We respected other people's homes. You could walk into anyone's home, if you were that way inclined, but no one did. Anyway we hadn't anything worth taking. Everyone was the same way, we were all barely getting by.

5

The lads at the corner would jeer at him when he passed. They were still idle, had no jobs and he was in the army. The British army.

6

There used to be lines in the yard. Rows of white sheets drying

7

During the war whenever a local man was killed or wounded the telegram boys used to come. One day my mother saw the telegram boy. She met him on the stairs. She almost fainted. But he passed her and went to another woman on the next floor.

8

We'd draw squares with chalk on the ground, with numbers in them 1, 2, 3, 4, 5, 6. We'd use a round, flatish empty tin. You'd throw it - if it landed on square 4 you hopped up into 4. Then you kicked it into the next number up - square 5. Then you hopped into 5 and tried to kick it into the next one. Depending on how many you were able to get you won.

Heirlooms & Hand-me-downs

These extracts were among 220 in total considered for inclusion on one of the final 21 plaques that now appear on the walls of buildings throughout Nicholas Street, Bride Street, Bride Road and the Rosser.

9.
Title: In His Latter Years
Page: 94

10.
Title: The Wash House
Page: 95

11.
Title: School Days
Page: 125

12.
Title: Relationships And The Flats
Page: 151

13.
Title: Living History
Page: 213

9 He carried a stick because of his wooden leg. He would shout, banging the railings and ground with his stick. You would hear the clanging. He would wave his stick around or raise it in mid-air. Then he started to swipe at people. That was how it effected him – the war.

13 This place has a history. But it's also a living thing. We are living in the here and now.

10 Of a Tuesday the women would be up washing their clothes in the wash house up beside the Iveagh market. You carried your washing up and washed it in the basins, put it into a boiler, put it in the rinser and then brought it up the wringer. The clothes were then put on the big steel horse to dry them.

11 We couldn't wait to get out of school because of the beatings we got. Corporal punishment. It was open season. It wasn't just the stick. In my school one teacher used the leg of a chair. Another had half a snooker cue. Another used a pole for opening windows.

12 When I got married I got a flat beside my Ma and Da's flat. My front room was next to my Da's front bedroom. When I had my fire lighting you could go into my Da's flat and into the front bedroom and put your hand on the wall. It would be roasting. I used to say to my Da that he owed me money for keeping his flat warm.

Heirlooms & Hand-me-downs

The Final 21 Plaques

My mother didn't believe in doctors. She couldn't afford to pay them anyway. All the mothers were the same. They had these old fashioned remedies. 'I'll cure you myself', my mother used to say.

17/158 Pg. 48

There was a chemical factory across the road. It went up in flames in the 1940's. It blazed for three days. They levelled it and turned it into a car park. My father worked there. Later they built flats on it.

Pg. 58

My father was in the British Army during the 1st World War. He got some medals but when he left the army he pawned them and never redeemed them. My brother, he was in the British Airforce during the 2nd World War. My father was mad to know about it. He used to say to my mother, 'I can't get a word out of him'. My brother got the Burma Star and all, but he never even wrote away for his medal. He said he didn't need medals to remind him.

9/28/34/35/158 Pg. 71

I went to 'The Metropole' on O'Connell Street for ballroom dancing, 'The Young Hearts' on the Adelaide Road for quick steps and waltzes and 'The Ierne' for céilí. I went to the 'Crystal Ballroom' off Grafton Street and to 'The Pallas' on O'Connell Street. Every Saturday night I'd dance at 'The Olympic Ballroom' off Pleasants Street. Fellas would ask me out to the pictures and I went with my pal to 'The Royal' every Friday and also to 'The Gaiety', 'The Olympia' and 'The Queens'. That was the late 1940's.

40/158 Pg. 75

They had seven children and decided this was enough. One day after mass, she arrived home and told her husband that the priest said no one of childbearing age should stop having children. Sometime later she had another. Both she and the baby died during the birth. They were buried together.

41/158 Pg. 76

The hill was steeper, the street narrower. The surface was all cobblestones. When winter weather made them freeze, horses struggled to climb. Sparks flew from their hooves.

Pg. 91

'Rags, rags, rags', he'd shout. The Ragman was a fella on a horse and cart, he'd have goldfish in little jars. He'd give you one if you brought down a good clover coat or some other article. Sometimes me Da noticed things missing and he'd lose the head. The Ragman always came of a Friday or Saturday morning - right, when he'd know your parents would be working or out getting messages. He'd come of a Tuesday as well because he'd know the women would be up washing their clothes in the wash house by the Iveagh market. He stopped coming around in 1967.

94/158 Pg. 133

From the time I was born Moggy was there. I'd be swinging on the lamp post (or scutting the back of the coal lorry) and she'd be sitting there at the window her dog beside her, watching the kids and the people. She had six kids herself and she was left a young widow. She'd wash the dead or anything to earn a shilling to rear them and if she never had a shilling she was always in good form. She'd go around for a few glasses of stout at Corbetts and would come around singing.

98/158 Pg. 140

There was six tenants up the hall and every neighbour would wash their flight down to the next woman underneath them and that woman would come out and wash the steps to the next one and so on. Everyone took their turn to wash the stairs and all.

107/158 Pg. 147

There was a toss school of a Sunday. Men would gather behind the Iveagh Baths which was our back yard. They'd have notes and coins in a pot on the ground in the middle of them. Side bets were taken as well. If you seen the cops coming you ran over shouting, 'Cops! Cops!', and the men all ran off. Occasionally I'd do that just to get the few bob left on the ground. The cops would be coming up the yard and they'd ask, 'What are you doing?' I'm hanging out the washing', I'd say and shake out the tea towel I kept over my shoulder.

105/109 Pg.
158   149

I ended up drinking in the same pub me Father drank in and today me son drinks there. The main thing in the small pubs was the camaraderie – the sing-song, the sense of humour. If you were looking for a fella to do something you wouldn't go to his house, you'd go to a pub. You'd ask where he drinks not where he lives. Many of the pubs around here are gone, such as O'Byrnes, O'Connells, Napper Tandy, Corbetts, Graces, Phelans . . .

113/145 Pg.
158   154

I never really had a conversation with my father. Sometime in the 1960's he caught me mitching from school and gave me an awful hiding. Ripped the clothes off me, lashed me with the belt and punched me in the eyes.

116 Pg.
158   156

During the 1980's there was still no hot water in the flats. I had to go round to the Iveagh for a bath. I'd pay a few pence and go upstairs. There were separate rooms where you had your bath. I'd go mostly of a Saturday. By times I'd meet people who were in the same predicament as myself.

129 Pg.
158   176

'Have you ever been on Methodone?' they asked. It was their way of asking me if I had ever taken drugs or was a drug addict. I was on Methodone - Yes, but I did have a good record of clean urine and letters from the doctor saying I was clean. We had maximum points and things looked good. So I told the truth.

140 Pg.
158   193

When he moved around here me father had gone blind. He hadn't a clue where he was. I used to bring him out onto the balcony and I used to say to him, 'Da, there's the yard where we used to hang out our washing'. But he was all confused. He couldn't make it out because there were no lines and no white sheets or other clothes hanging from them. It was a different yard.

144 Pg.
158   200

I'd be standing in the kitchen cooking my breakfast. I'd pull up the blinds and open the window to let air in. Next thing you see someone gawking in, waving in and taking snaps. Hello, one says. How are you sir? Good, I says. Would you like a rasher sandwich?

Pg.
202

We could have moved somewhere else. But why? We have been here so long that this is our home.

146 Pg.
158   203

The renovation was completed in September 2000. But if you don't maintain a place it will fall into disrepair and over time the people living there will become demoralised. The place will then go back to the way it was before.

150 Pg.
158   207

It would be good if a community centre could be built here. Even if one of the flats was put aside for it. Somewhere for the kids to go at night. It could be nice if some sort of football pitch could be built into one of the yards. Maybe more trees could be planted.

Pg.
210

If you really love something and you have it – then no matter what it is, I think you deserve it. We are only caretakers for the things we have. I am lucky to have this flat. It is all I really have and I really adore it. I think I take care of it the best I can.

154 Pg.
158   214

Chris Reid completed a public artwork consisting of 20 bronze plaques and a printed book. The texts are based on recordings the artist made from 2004 to 2008 with residents and people associated with Nicholas Street, Ross Road, Bride Street and Bride Road. Chris Reid was commissioned through Dublin City Council's Public Art programme, arising from the refurbishment of these buildings and funded by the Department of the Environment, Heritage and Local Government.

Heirlooms & Hand-me-downs

Credits

I would like to thank all the participants who spoke to me, let me include images from their personal collections and also helped me to edit the final work.

Rita Behan	Eddie Hatton	Pat Nash
Harriet Dalton (Connaughton)	Kieran Kavanagh (Dublin City	Mary Nicholson Marian Nolan
Harriet Donnelly	Architects Division)	Fran O'Connor
John Freer	Anne Kelly	James O'Keefe
John Freer (senior)	Carol Keogh	Lilly O'Reilly
Patrick Freer	Andrew Kerfoot	Michael O'Sullivan
Steve Freer	Margaret Kerfoot	Fergus Redmond
John Gallagher	Daniel Lyons	Margaret Slyman
Marian Glennon	Leo Magee	Margaret Taylor
James Gough	Tony May	Paul Tracy
Maureen Gough	Aileen Morrissey	Siobhan VanDekeere
Christopher Halpin	Mary Murtagh	Aidan Walsh
Christopher Halpin (Senior)		

I would like to thank all those participants who have chosen to remain anonymous.

Acknowledgements

There are many people who have supported the production of this book. Without the support and backing of a number of individuals and organisations, *Heirlooms and Hand-me-downs* would not have seen the light of day in the form in which it comes to you.

First and foremost, sincere thanks must go to all the contributors who made the book possible and generously shared their experiences, stories, photos and other material. A particular thanks is due to Ruairí Ó Cuív and Sinéad Connolly at Dublin City Council; Sarah Tuck at Create and Declan McGonagle at NCAD.

Special thanks also to: Zinc Design Consultants; Rosaleen Regan and Anne Carroll at Audiotrans for transcribing many mini discs; Catherine Aylmer for additional transcription; Emma Sherry for proofreading; Sarah Tuck and Katrina Goldstone at Create, additional editing; and to Jim Reid for lifts and holding the ladder.

Archives, Museums, Libraries and Other Institutions
Thanks to Glen Dunne at The National Library of Ireland; Colum O' Riordan at The Irish Architectural Archive; Natalie Milne at the RTÉ Stills Library; Nancy Costello, Ordnance Survey Ireland; Elbhlin Roche, Guinness Archive, Diageo Ireland; Anne-Marie Ryan, Kilmainham Gaol Museum; Michael Molloy, Digital Library, Dublin City Library and Archive; John Kearney, Offaly Historical and Archaeological Society; Brother Edmund Garvey and archivist Karen Johnson, Christian Brothers Province Centre; Paola Catizone (Dublin Memories Project); Ronan Teevan, Caxton Antique Prints.

Thanks to Jim and Ed at Inspirational Arts for high resolution scanning and image consultation. Thanks to Bronze Art for casting and installing the plaques.

While Chris Reid has taken care in collecting all the information for this book and in preparing the printed publication, he does not assume, and hereby disclaims, any liability for errors and omissions.